ELT IN CONTEXT

SERIES EDITOR, **ANDY CL**

C000186271

PERSPECTIVES ON

TEACHING
ENGLISH
in a
BINATIONAL
CENTER in
BRAZIL

ISABELA VILLAS BOAS and KATY COX

tesolpress

Design and layout by Capitol Communications, LLC, Crofton, Maryland USA
and printed by Gasch Printing, LLC, Odenton, Maryland USA

TESOL Press
TESOL International Association
1925 Ballenger Avenue
Alexandria, Virginia 22314 USA
www.tesol.org

Senior Manager, Publications: Myrna Jacobs
Cover Design: Citrine Sky Design, Edgewater, Maryland USA
Copyeditor: Sarah J. Duffy

TESOL Book Publications Committee
   Robyn L. Brinks Lockwood, Chair
   Elizabeth Byleen
   Margo DelliCarpini
   Robert Freeman
   Deoksoon Kim
   Ilka Kostka
   Guofang Li
   John Liontas, Past Chair
   Gilda Martinez-Alba
   Allison Rainville
   Jason Stegemoller
   Adrian J. Wurr

ISBN 9781942223696
Library of Congress Control Number 2015942166

Contents

Series Editor's Preface

In September 2008, *The Guardian* newspaper in England described David Foster Wallace as "the most brilliant writer of his generation." In its tribute to him, following his death by suicide at the age of 46, *The Guardian* presented a now well-known story that Wallace told at the beginning of his commencement speech to a graduating class at Kenyon College in Ohio:

> There are these two young fish swimming along, and they happen to meet an older fish swimming the other way, who nods at them and says, "Morning, boys, how's the water?" And the two young fish swim on for a bit, and then eventually one of them looks over at the other and goes, "What the hell is water?" (para. 1)

That water is what this series is about. As Wallace's story illustrates so eloquently and so succinctly, when we are immersed in our context all the time, we stop noticing what we are surrounded by. Or if we were aware of it at some point in the past, we stopped noticing it some time ago. Wallace went on to explain that "the immediate point of the fish story is that the most obvious, ubiquitous, important realities are often the ones that are the hardest to see and talk about" (para. 2).

The writers in this series were asked to step back from the English language teaching (ELT) and learning contexts that they are most familiar with and look at those contexts with fresh eyes. But why do this? There are many reasons for reflecting on, exploring, and writing about our contexts, one of the most important of which relates to what we do every day as TESOL professionals and how we do it. As Diane Larsen-Freeman (2000) puts it,

> a method is decontextualized. How a method is implemented in the classroom is going to be affected not only by who the teacher is, but also who the students are, the students' and their teacher's expectations of appropriate social roles, the institutional constraints and demands, and factors connected to the wider sociocultural context in which the instruction takes place. (p. x)

v

It is that wider context that we are exploring in this series.

To enable them to step back from contexts they are so familiar with, each writer was asked to follow a template, starting with the notion that individuals are a context in and of themselves. Therefore, in Chapter 1, the writers introduce themselves to the readers and explain how they came to be where they are now, doing what they do as, as TESOL professionals. This also helps address the notions of objectivity and subjectivity, as we cannot be objective about ourselves or those things we care about, have an opinion on, know well, and so on. All we can do is to be as objective as we can be about our own subjectivities, which is another function of the first chapter.

In Chapter 2, the authors summarize English language teaching and learning at the national level in their country, with a focus on the level of learners they are working with (e.g., students at the college or university level). Chapter 3 looks at ELT at the local level in each country, and Chapter 4 describes the particular language teaching and learning organization (LTO) where the authors work. To help our readers get as deep an understanding of the context as possible, the Chapters 5 and 6 present "A Day in the Life of a Teacher" and "A Day in the Life of a Learner" at the authors' LTOs. We realize, of course, that there is no "typical" teacher or learner, as everyone is unique. So a composite of a number of teachers and learners is presented in each of those chapters, to help readers walk in the shoes of those in the LTO and to give readers a strong sense of the day-to-day realities of life inside and outside the LTO, which are often not written about, published, or presented.

In terms of context, having moved from the national and local levels to the institutional and individual levels, the authors were asked to go back to The Big Picture, using the focus question: What could readers from other LTOs, that are like yours but that are in another context or country, learn that would help them in their daily work in their own context or country? For example, if the book is about working with adult learners in one part of the Arabic-speaking world, what could TESOL professionals working with adults in other Arabic-speaking parts of the world learn from reading the book that would help them in their particular context? Or what could readers working with adult Arabic-speaking students outside the Arabic-speaking world (e.g., in the United States) learn that would help them? In the final chapter, the authors were asked to give a brief reflective account of what they learned from writing the book, about their own context and about the contexts of others.

These books are also aimed at TESOL professionals who are considering working in LTOs in the contexts and countries described in the series and who need a clear, concise, and up-to-date account of what it is like to live and work there. One of the challenges of doing that is the fact that teaching and learning contexts are changing all the time, some more quickly and more dramatically than others. However, taking that constraint into account, our goal has been to create a series of books that remind us of the importance of the professional waters in which we swim every day, and to help prepare those who may wish to join us in these particular English language teaching and learning contexts.

Andy Curtis, PhD
President, TESOL International Association (2015–2016)

References

Larsen-Freeman, D. (2000). *Techniques and principles in language teaching* (2nd ed.). New York, NY: Oxford University Press.

Wallace, D. F. (2008, September 19). Plain old untrendy troubles and emotions. *The Guardian.* Retrieved from http://www.theguardian.com

Introduction

In 1976, the British Council published one of its *English Language Teaching Profiles* on Brazil. At that time, the writers of the 16-page booklet noted:

> In 1968 the Brazilian government launched major university reforms, and the situation is still fluid. Portuguese is the official language of Brazil and English is learned as a foreign language for international communication, occasionally as a medium of instruction, as a tool for study and academic and professional advancement, and for certain cultural, social and prestige purposes. (p. 1)

In many ways, the situation in Brazil today is still "fluid"—economically, socially and politically—and English is still seen as a tool for advancement as well as for the purposes of prestige.

In terms of English language teaching (ELT) in Brazil today, it is interesting to see what has changed and what remains much the same since the British Council published its booklet 40 years ago. For example, today, as in 1976, "the value of English as an acquired skill is enormous, and it is the most frequently taught foreign language" (p. 1). The historical snapshot also noted that "the most effective English teaching occurs outside the school system in the private sector" (p. 1). According to the authors of this book in the ELT In Context series, Isabela Villas Boas and Katy Cox, that last statement is also still true. In this book, the reasons for it still being true after four decades are presented and discussed in relation to Brazil's private, nonprofit language teaching and learning sector.

In many contexts, *private* and *for profit* are connoted, in the same way that *public* and *nonprofit* are similarly associated. However, in Brazil, as in some other contexts, it is possible that one of the most important and influential developments in ELT in the past 40 to 50 years has been the establishment and growth of private, nonprofit language teaching and learning organizations (LTOs). It is also possible that such LTOs—when run professionally and pedagogically well—can bring together the best of both worlds, privately funded and publically available language education.

Nearly 20 years after the British Council booklet was published, Palo Kol and Steve Stoynoff (1995) published "A Status Report on English Language Teaching Brazil" as part of a series titled TESOL Around the World. Kol and Stoynoff concluded that "there are large differences between teachers employed in public schools and those employed in private language academies in terms of quality of language education" (p. 5). According Boas and Cox, that is another statement that remains largely true. Therefore, some important questions to ask are: Why are such statements still true after all this time, and after so much else has changed in Brazil during that time? What has improved? What still needs to happen? Boas and Cox give a number of insights that help answer those, and other, questions.

Moving from ELT in Brazil in 1976 and 1995 to more recently, in 2010, the *Brazilian English Language Teaching Journal* was launched, which showed how far ELT in Brazil had come, from the brief booklets and one-page reports of the 1970s and 1990s to an online journal focused specifically on ELT in Brazil. It is worth noting that the first article in the first volume of the *Brazilian English Language Teaching Journal*, by Everton Vinicius de Santa (2010), was titled "Foreign Teacher Education and Its Influences Under the Light of Autobiographic Narratives." In the introduction to the article, de Santa states:

> In the process of teaching/learning a second language, educators' beliefs act meaningfully in their performance, in their pedagogical choices, and in the student/educator interaction. These beliefs can be modified over new experiences, since during his or her undergraduate course, the student-teachers have the opportunity to experience many different school settings. (p. 5)

Although this book is not about foreign language teacher education in Brazil, there is a strong element of "autobiographic narrative" in this book, as there is in all the books in this ELT In Context series. This is deliberate, as one of the distinctive contributions this series aims to make is to put the context and the writers at center of the series, as opposed to other books that focus on the methodologies, materials, technologies, postcolonial politics, and positioning of ELT. Those aspects of ELT do appear, however, in one form or another, in all of the books in this series. But instead of simply paying lip service to the importance of context, and instead of obscuring the writers in an attempt to present the writings as being objective in some pseudoscientific fashion, we have deliberately and purposefully placed the context and the writers' experiences of that context at the center of these books.

In July 2015, the five countries forming the BRICS groups of emerging national economies held their seventh summit. The original four countries in that group—Brazil, Russia, India and China—were joined by South Africa in

2010. The population of those five countries is approaching 3 billion, which is nearly 40% of the entire world's population. As part of the BRICS group, the first meeting of which was in 2006, Brazil has continued, and will continue, to play an increasingly important role in the new world order, which means that English will also continue to grow in Brazil. Therefore, for anyone interested in learning more about ELT in the world's fifth-largest country, both by geographical area and by population, this book will serve as a clear, concise, and up-to-date guide.

Andy Curtis, PhD
Graduate School of Education, Anaheim University, California, USA

References

British Council. (1976). *English language teaching profile: Brazil.* London, England: British Council, English-Teaching Information Centre.

de Santa, E. V. (2010). Foreign teacher education and its influences under the light of autobiographic narratives. *Brazilian English Language Teaching Journal, 1*(1), 5–13.

Kol, P., & Stoynoff, S. (1995). A status report on English language teaching Brazil. *Linguistics and Language Behavior Abstracts, 5*(5).

1

The Individual as Context

Isabela Villas Boas

Teaching English was not on my career list. In fact, ever since I was a small child, I had wanted to be a journalist because I liked reading and writing. I became an English as a foreign language (EFL) teacher in Brazil by accident, or—some might say—by destiny.

In 1974, when I was only 8 years old, my family moved to the United States for my father to pursue a master's degree and a doctorate. I had never learned English and was enrolled in the third grade of an elementary school in a suburb of Houston, Texas, where I learned English in a full immersion situation. The 3-year experience in the United States shaped who I am in ways that I came to understand only many years later.

Upon arriving back in Brazil in 1978, as my parents did not want me to forget the English I had learned so well, they enrolled me in a traditional English language teaching (ELT) institute in Brasília, Casa Thomas Jefferson (CTJ), a Brazil-U.S. binational center. I was only 11, so though I was quite proficient, but I was not mature enough to take an advanced course, so I was placed in the intermediate level. I went through the whole program at CTJ and took several post-advanced courses there before I was 18 and able to enroll in the teacher training course (TTC), the only one in the institution that I hadn't taken. My goal in taking the TTC was to advance my studies in English, not be a teacher.

The same year I started TTC, 1985, I also entered college to study translation, but soon transferred to journalism. On a Sunday night a year and a half later, I received a call from my first TTC teacher, Katy Cox, inviting me to teach at Casa Thomas Jefferson. At that time the institution was much smaller and hired inexperienced teachers like me. I loved CTJ and decided to give it a try, at least while I was still in college.

In 1990, I graduated from college and got a part-time job at a local newspaper. My goal was to finish the year at CTJ and then resign to pursue a career as a journalist. However, at the end of the year, Katy invited me to be a course supervisor, which I happily accepted. I had hated the experience at the local newspaper and had found the work environment terrible, compared to the wonderful environment at CTJ.

The next few years were dedicated to becoming a true professional in the ELT field. That was when I started attending conferences, including my first TESOL Convention in Long Beach, 1995, and also began teaching methodology in TTC, which I prepared for by way of self-study, reading the major reference books in ELT methodology available at that time.

In 1998, after 6 years as a course supervisor and 1 as a pedagogical counselor, I decided to invest in my EFL career and pursue a master's degree. My husband, who had been my student at CTJ, had always wanted to live in the United States, so I applied to three universities there, received a Graduate Tuition Scholarship from Arizona State University, and thus moved to Tempe, Arizona, with my husband and two small children, who were 2 and 6 years of age. During my studies in the United States, I always had CTJ in mind. All of my end-of-term papers were written with my local audience in mind and published in the *CTJ Journal*. For my applied project, I managed to reconcile my interest in writing with my career as an ELT professional, and I wrote about implementing a portfolio system in our writing courses.

Back to CTJ in 2000, I soon became a consultant to the general academic coordinator, Katy Cox, and was appointed the general supervisor, responsible for providing methodological orientation to all course supervisors. I continued investing in my ongoing professional development by attending and presenting at local, national, and international conferences, especially the TESOL Convention.

In 2005 I decided to take a further step and pursue a doctorate in education, as there isn't an applied linguistics program at the local university (Universidade de Brasília) and my family situation did not favor another major relocation. However, since there was a literacy strand in the program and my advisor had been a professor in the Linguistics Department for 25 years, I was able to continue focusing on second language writing.

In 2007, Katy decided to step down from her position as general academic coordinator and appointed me as her successor. She became a consultant for CTJ and was responsible for the mentoring of newly hired teachers, together with two other senior colleagues. More important than that, she became and still is my mentor. Two years ago the title of my position was changed to academic superintendent, but the job didn't change. I oversee CTJ's academic program, comprising over 17,000 students and 260 teachers.

Katy Cox

All through my elementary, high school, and undergraduate years of schooling, most of which took place in California, I adored school. I enjoyed vacation periods but was always more than ready to get back into the rhythm and the social energy generated by being in classes, being with friends, coping with the goals implicit in carrying out assignments, studying for tests, and so on. My parents were unrepentant roamers, always moving from place to place in various states and cities, and the one predictable dimension in my life, no matter where we were, was school. However, the one thing I never wanted to be—professionally—was a teacher. I had such a tendency to admire my teachers that their shoes seemed impossible to fill. I thought it would be safer to be *anything* else.

In my undergraduate studies, my greatest love—in spite of the fact that I began my studies majoring in journalism—was literature (British, Russian, European; plays, novels, poetry) and the subject I most abhorred was Spanish (a requirement for all college students in California at the time). A lover of language, I hated the feeling of linguistic incapacity inherent in all that "foreignness," the sensation of being an infant in adult clothing. My area of maximum confidence was in the teacher-avoidance strategies I had perfected throughout semesters of foreign language "study." This peculiar talent and my awareness of how foreign language study can affect a reasonably intelligent and normally enthusiastic student would stand me in good stead much later on, as you will see.

Time passed, and in my last semesters of study, in connection with the literature dimension, I was called on to tutor some Korean students whose efforts to pass their required Shakespeare course were leading them to nearly suicidal levels of failure. My reputation as a helper (not a teacher, mind you) was definitely boosted by the ultimate success of my "students," and through some fairly circuitous circumstances, I followed up college graduation by becoming the director of the San Jose campus Foreign Student Association and its conglomeration of volunteers. Within a year, I was persuaded to enter the TEFL/TESL master's program in San Francisco State University. One year into that study, in 1968, I was invited to teach in the American Language Institute, which was operational for foreign students attempting to study at the university level in the United States. I was also in charge of volunteer ESL teachers at the city's International Center, struggling to give them orientation with regard to use of materials and constructive teaching attitudes.

The master's program also included teaching classes in the city's Italian district and to migrant workers employed in the city's surrounding agricultural areas. The combination of all these engagements—coupled with the theoretical study focuses which were regular course requirements—provided a dynamically dense foundation of techniques and attitudes, which would connect me effectively to a kaleidoscope of nationalities and needs in the large collective of students for whom I felt at least partially responsible.

With an MA to my credit, in 1968, I found employment at the San Francisco Alemany Adult School and spent 3 years greatly enjoying helping foreigners from many nationalities and backgrounds integrate (linguistically at least) into surroundings very far from their original homes. I was not inclined to leave this gratifying situation, but a good friend and former MA colleague thought we should put our skills to use overseas, even if only for the time it took to get the sense of other teaching dimensions. The result of a good deal of insistent persuasion was that I applied for a 1-year stint as a United States Information Service Fellow in one of the Latin American countries wishing to participate in this program. In 1971 I was sent a take-it-or-leave-it contract to teach at the (then) small binational center in Brasilia, Brazil.

On July 25 of that year, I landed on the high, dry plateau of a fledgling capitol city and began—unbeknownst to me—the rest of my life there. In the more than 40 years since, I have taught nearly all levels and held the position of assistant coordinator with four different general academic coordinators, twice refusing directorial invitations to assume the coordinator's position because I didn't feel I had acquired the managerial maturity to capably meet its demands. I finally took the plunge and held the position of general academic coordinator (now known as academic superintendent) for 17 years. For the last 7 years, I have been part of an academic consultancy firm that assists in training incoming CTJ teachers and conducts observations of more senior teachers as part of an ongoing performance assessment for teachers across the board.

In all of these situations, I have participated in a wide variety of projects— story adaptation, basic sentences illustration, test writing, conception and refinement of observation and evaluation instruments, to mention a few. I have participated in training programs related to book adoption on behalf of more than one textbook publisher, and in several other binational centers in other Brazilian states. And I have given academic presentations in numerous EFL centers and in international TESOL conferences. I can say—going back to my insecurities as a language student—that my empathy with "foreign-ness," my willingness to be pushed by unexpected winds into various ports of discovery, my gratitude for good friends and finally finding a real home all have made it possible to make a positive contribution to my institute and to the profession from which I still derive profound pleasure.

English Language Teaching and Learning at the National Level in Brazil

Brazil is a large country in South America where Portuguese is spoken. Though the vast majority of the countries in South America speak Spanish, due to the political and economic hegemony of Great Britain in the 19th century and of the United States since World War II, in Brazil English is regarded as the most important foreign language to learn, for professional and academic purposes. Nevertheless, still relatively few people in the country are proficient in English. According to EF Education First's (n.d.) English Proficiency Index, Brazil ranks 31st among the 44 countries studied, and its speakers are classified by the Index as having "low proficiency," on average. Likewise, in a survey conducted by Global English Corporation, Brazil scored below 4 on a business English proficiency scale of 1 to 10 (Rapoza, 2012).

In 2012, the Brazilian government launched a program called Science Without Borders, aimed at sending around 100,000 university students in the STEM areas of science, technology, engineering, and math to renowned universities around the world for a 1-year study period. The U.S. government was one of the first to operationalize this project with its country's universities, but the government was unable to fill all the openings for courses in the United States and other English-speaking countries due to the lack of students proficient enough to engage in academic studies in English. Thus, despite its growing importance in the world economy, Brazil still lacks competitiveness when it comes to the English proficiency of its academia and workforce.

With few exceptions, given these indicators, we can safely say that the teaching of English as a foreign language in Brazil has not been effective at the primary, secondary, and tertiary levels, resulting in the need for learners of all ages seeking proficiency in English to enroll in private English language teaching (ELT) institutes such as Casa Thomas Jefferson. In order to explain how this came to be, this chapter provides a brief history of ELT in Brazil and discusses the current state of this developing field in the country.

A Brief History of ELT in Primary and Secondary Schools in Brazil

There are historical reasons for this current state of low proficiency in Brazil, as the teaching of English has been inconsistent and inadequate since it became mandatory in 1809, when the Portuguese king Don João VI came to Brazil fleeing Napoleon's army and introduced English and French in schools (Santos, 2011). Though the purpose of teaching the two modern languages was to enable students to communicate orally and in writing, the grammar-translation method was adopted, as it was the only known method at the time (Lima, 2009, as cited in Santos, 2011).

It was only in 1931, one year after the creation of the Ministry of Education, that a government decree stipulated the direct method for the teaching of foreign languages (Machado, Campos, & Saunders, 2007). That was successfully implemented in the first Brazilian secondary school, Colégio Pedro II, founded in 1937 in Rio de Janeiro, through the hiring of proficient teachers and the adoption of new materials (Chagas, 1957, as cited in Leffa, 1999). However, the limited number of hours and the lack of proficient teachers made it impossible to implement the direct method on a wider scale (Chagas, as cited in Machado et al., 2007). It is important to note that Colégio Pedro II included 7 years of French, 5 of English, and 3 of German in its curriculum, showing the strong emphasis on foreign language teaching at that time.

A secondary school reform in 1942 created two high school cycles (*Ginasial* and *Colegial*). The first cycle included Latin, French, and English, while the second focused on French, English, and Spanish. Again, official documents and decrees stipulated the use of the direct method, but these recommendations never functionally reached the classrooms, where "read and translate" continued to be the method used (Leffa, 1999). Leffa (1999) considers the 1942 reform the golden age of the teaching of foreign languages in Brazil, when all students learned Latin, French, English, and Spanish and many graduated from secondary school able to read original literature in these languages. French was still the preferred language, with more teaching hours, but English slowly made its way to become the most important foreign language due to the greater international prominence of the United States after World War II and the growth of Brazil's economic dependence on the United States (Paiva, 2003).

In 1961, a new regulatory bill for education, Lei de Diretrizes e Bases, decentralized education in Brazil and transferred to state education councils the decision whether to include a foreign language in their curricula. Ten years later, a second Lei de Diretrizes e Bases reduced the number of school years from 12 to 11 and emphasized the need for secondary schools to prepare students for the workplace, reducing the number of hours dedicated to foreign languages. Many primary schools eliminated foreign languages from their curricula, and many secondary schools reduced them to 1 hour a week, sometimes only in the first year. As a result, many students went through school during that period without ever having studied a foreign language (Leffa, 1999). Paradoxically, English was becoming more and more popular, and the affluent enrolled in private English language teaching institutes to learn the language, originating the longstanding belief that one cannot learn English effectively in regular schools in Brazil (Paiva, 2003). In 1976, the teaching of a foreign language was again made mandatory in secondary schools.

In December 1996, a third version of the Lei de Diretrizes e Bases was passed and the teaching of a foreign language became mandatory from fifth grade on. The foreign language in question could be chosen by the school community, and English was the choice in the vast majority of schools. One month earlier, the Brazilian Association of Applied Linguistics held a conference in the city of Florianopolis that produced the Letter of Florianopolis, demanding an immediate plan to reinstate the effective teaching of foreign languages in the country. According to Almeida Filho (2003), this conference introduced the academic discussion in Brazil regarding the need to change the focus of ELT from language structures to language notions and functions. From then on, the field of applied linguistics was established in Brazil, together with associations and annual events. Almeida Filho was the first applied linguist to propose communicative language teaching in Brazil.

However, what seemed to finally be an advancement in the teaching of foreign languages in regular schools resulted in the continuation of the traditionally adopted approach, as the 1998 Curricular Standards for the Teaching of Foreign Languages in Primary Schools, published by the Ministry of Education, minimized the importance of teaching oral skills. The report argued that very few Brazilians had the opportunity to engage in oral interactions with native speakers of the languages learned, making the teaching of oral skills socially irrelevant. Also, the document stated that the lack of material conditions, the number of students in the classroom, and the insufficient number of proficient teachers made a reading approach more viable.

According to Paiva (2003), these standards contributed to perpetuating the gap between public school students and those who could afford to enroll in a private language institute. Rather than seeking solutions to the problems mentioned above and improving foreign language teaching in public schools, the document merely accepted the low standards and the impossibility of improving them. Other public policies reinforced the disregard for the learning of foreign languages in regular schools, such as the exclusion of foreign language textbooks in the country's textbook selection and distribution policy, which was finally implemented only in 2011 (Santos, 2011), and the absence of foreign languages in the first versions of the Exame Nacional do Ensino Médio (National Secondary School Exam).

Though the teaching of English in private schools is generally more substantial than in public schools, even in most of the private schools the focus is still restricted to grammar explanations, the reading of short, simple texts, and an emphasis on multiple-choice exercises similar to the ones encountered in university admission exams (Santos, 2011). Classes are large and heterogeneous, and instruction is mostly in the students' native language, Brazilian Portuguese. Only in recent years have regular schools adopted materials from international publishers, some of which were specifically developed for the Brazilian public and private school population, as opposed to those developed for private ELT institutes, and authored or coauthored by Brazilian ELT professionals.

As Brazilian universities and colleges have apparently not been able to prepare foreign language teachers effectively, the lack of qualified teachers has contributed to the poor EFL instruction in primary and secondary schools. Few of the students who get into university to study language arts are proficient in English, so they count on learning the language during their university studies. However, the overly theoretical curriculum and the number of hours dedicated to learning English per se make it very difficult for such future teachers to achieve a level higher than intermediate. These teachers are also pedagogically unprepared, as the curriculum does not emphasize the more practical aspects of teaching (Cox & Assis-Peterson, 2008).

ELT at the Tertiary Level in Brazil

English is widely taught at the tertiary level using an English for specific purposes approach called *Inglês instrumental* (instrumental English). This approach was promoted by the prominent Brazilian applied linguist Maria Antonieta Celani, based on the emerging need in the late 1970s for university students to read academic texts in their fields of study. Celani led a national project, with the support of the British Council, the Ministry of Education, and U.S. and British linguists, which resulted in the training of teachers, development of materials, and creation of a national resource center, now called Centro de Pesquisas, Recursos e Informação em Leitura (Research, Resource, and Information Center on Reading). The instrumental English approach focuses on developing reading strategies in specific fields of study. Grammar is taught in context and as a means to help reading comprehension, and the vocabulary of students' specific field of study is emphasized (Ferreira & Rosa, 2008).

Nowadays, instrumental English is adopted in most universities and technical schools in Brazil as well as in preparatory courses for university and public service entrance exams. The aim is to develop effective readers, so speaking is not focused on at all, and classes can be taught in the students' native language. As a result, with the exception of those studying language arts and preparing to be English language teachers, university students in general do not take EFL classes aimed at developing communicative competence as a whole and using the four skills in academic and professional settings. Once again, those who want to fully develop their proficiency in English usually have to enroll in private language institutes. Many federal and state universities in Brazil also offer English and other foreign languages in language centers run by the universities themselves and for which students have to pay tuition.

The Emergence of Binational Centers in Brazil

As shown in the brief history above, it was in the 1930s that secondary schools were officially created in Brazil, and along with this development came the inclusion of EFL in the curriculum, due to the growing political and economic importance of the language. As the United States turned its attention to Brazil, and President Franklin D. Roosevelt, elected in 1933, announced a new era for Latin America, more and more people turned their attention to English rather than French, up to then the foreign language of preference of the Brazilian elite. This resulted in the growing desire of middle-class people to learn English effectively (M. O. Nogueira, 2010). This political and economic scenario led to the opening of the first private ELT institutes in the country, supported by both the British and U.S. governments.

In 1934, with the support of the British Embassy in Brazil, the Brazilian Society of British Culture (Associação Brasileira de Cultura Inglesa) opened its doors in Rio de Janeiro. One year later, another Cultura Inglesa was opened in São Paulo (M. C. B. Nogueira, 2007), soon followed by the first binational center in Brazil, Instituto Brasil-Estados Unidos (IBEU; Brazil-United States Institute), founded in 1937 in Rio de Janeiro, the capital of Brazil at that time. The idea of creating a binational cultural institution had been launched 3 years earlier by Professor Stephan Duggan, of the International Institute of Education in New York. IBEU was opened with the support of prominent Brazilian public figures, and its first assembly was held in the Itamaraty Palace (Foreign Relations Ministry) with over 100 participants. The U.S. Embassy donated teaching materials and publications to the center and organized teacher training and scholarship programs. Having started with two teachers and eighteen students in 1937, in 1942 IBEU created its Language Teaching Department and was running regular courses in EFL and Portuguese for foreigners, as well as English for specific purposes for doctors, aviators, and nurses (M. O. Nogueira, 2010).

One year later, in 1938, reacting against the growing influence of nationalist Germany, especially in the south of Brazil, a group of intellectuals, among whom was the prominent writer Erico Veríssimo, created the Instituto Cultural Brasil-Norte Americano (Brazil-North American Cultural Institute) in Porto Alegre, with the support of the U.S. Embassy. For many years the center focused on cultural activities only, but with the lack of proficiency in English in the community, a language department was created in 1943 and the first ELT institute in the south of the country opened its doors (M. O. Nogueira, 2010).

In the same year, the first binational center in São Paulo was inaugurated, União Cultural Brasil-Estados Unidos (Brazil-USA Cultural Union). Soon after, binational centers were founded in various locations, such as Associação Cultural Brasil-Estados Unidos Salvador and Interamericano Curitiba, in 1941, IBEU Fortaleza, in 1943, and CCBEU Belém, in 1955, among many others. Casa Thomas Jefferson was opened in 1963 in Brasília, 3 years after the foundation of the city.

There are currently around 62 Brazil-U.S. binational centers in the country, focusing on the teaching of EFL but also on strengthening the ties between Brazil and the United States by giving the local community access to resource centers with publications in English, Education USA advising offices, and cultural programs. However, these binational centers are all independent and each one has its individual characteristics based on why and how it was created. Most binational centers are part of an Association of Binational Centers in Brazil (Coligação dos Centros Binacionais). This association has the mission of strengthening ties among the various centers and promoting the exchange of ideas regarding academic and administrative issues. The U.S. Embassy also certifies binational centers according to a set of required standards that encompass contemporary practices related to school administration, ELT, teacher development, provision of resources on U.S. culture, and advising for studies in the United States.

Binational centers are institutions that are particularly focused on the quality of ELT services provided to the community and where academic excellence supersedes merely commercial interests. This can be attributed to the history of the creation of binational centers, the fact that most of them are nonprofit and run by an assembly and a board of directors, the academic and administrative support provided by the U.S. Embassy, and the need for accountability resulting from that support. However, the fierce competition from other ELT institutes in general, especially franchises, has forced binational centers to adopt contemporary management and marketing strategies to remain competitive in a diverse market in which the population is bombarded by false promises of becoming proficient in English in a year or so.

Responding to the market's needs, binational centers have expanded their programs and diversified their services, offering EFL classes to all ages and proficiency levels, from very young learners to seniors, beginners to post-advanced. Many have also included online learning in their portfolios, including Casa Thomas Jefferson, Ibeu (Rio), and Alumni (São Paulo).

One of the greatest challenges faced by binational centers today is the lack of qualified teachers. On the one hand, many certified teachers lack the advanced English skills required to teach in these institutions. On the other, there are highly proficient or native-English-speaking teaching candidates with degrees in other fields of study. The solution found by many binational centers is to provide the latter with in-house training through teacher training courses; doing so more easily and quickly provides methodological training to proficient candidates with degrees in other fields of study than taking certified teachers from an intermediate to a post-advanced level. It is worth highlighting that it is difficult to hire native speakers in Brazil, as most candidates do not have a work permit.

The Emergence of Other ELT Institutes in the Country

The ineffectiveness of foreign language teaching in the majority of schools and the growing demand for English proficiency led to the proliferation of commercial franchises starting in the 1960s (Schutz, 1999, as cited in M. C. B. Nogueira, 2007), which are still expanding. Nogueira (2007) classifies private ELT institutes into four categories:

- Binational centers: less commercial and more concerned with quality
- Franchises: invest heavily in advertising and emphasize their prefabricated materials and lesson plans, restricting expression of teachers' personal qualities and creativity
- Independent schools: usually run by former franchise owners
- Large institutes: operate similarly to binational centers, but do not have the connection to the U.S. State Department or the British Council, as typical binational centers do

Nowadays there are over 6,000 branches of around 70 different ELT institutes in the country (Azaredo, 2014), many of which are franchises, and the market has grown steadily in recent years due to an emerging Brazilian middle class, called *C class*. The term *C class* is used in Brazil to refer to the more than 35 million Brazilians who have moved out of poverty and into the ranks of the consuming masses in the past decade (Rathbone, 2014). Another aspect that has recently influenced the growth of the ELT market in Brazil are two major sports events held in the country: the World Cup in 2014 and the Olympics in 2016 (Moreira, 2010). The earnings of language teaching franchises in Brazil reached R$100 billion in 2012, approximately US$45 billion (de Jesus, 2013). There are franchises that specialize in teaching young learners, while others focus on teaching adults. Adult students, in particular, seek short-term, flexible programs.

Many franchises maximize their earnings by producing their own materials and investing little in qualified professionals, as they adopt their own prescriptive methods and provide teachers with detailed lesson plans. Thus, ELT is a profitable and growing business in the country, providing many opportunities for English teachers. However, there are not enough proficient and qualified teachers to fill all the available positions, and hiring qualified native speakers is a hindrance due to Brazil's rigid foreign labor laws.

New Directions in ELT at the Primary, Secondary, and Tertiary Levels

In the past 15 years or so, some private schools have sought alternatives to the traditional English taught in 50-minute classes twice a week to large, heterogeneous groups; they have either partnered with private language institutes or created their own language institutes. This model replicates the favorable conditions encountered in private ELT institutes, with at least 3 hours of instruction a week, students distributed among different levels according to their proficiency, smaller groups (15–20 students rather than 30–35), a communicative curriculum focusing on the four skills, and linguistically and methodologically proficient teachers. In some cases, this service is offered within the school curriculum, in lieu of the traditional English class. In others, it is offered in addition to the traditional English class, in an afterschool program. Though the Brazilian government has a plan to make all schools full time in the future, so far there are few public or private schools with a full-time curriculum. In the current part-time education system, children attend 4–5 hours of classes a day, and the school year comprises at least 200 mandatory days. The norm in most private schools is that students take their regular classes either in the morning or in the afternoon only and, in the other period, engage in extracurricular activities for which parents have to pay additional tuition.

Another way of guaranteeing the early development of children's proficiency in English is enrolling them in international or bilingual schools. Though these schools have existed in the country for many years, their very high tuition fees have made them accessible to upper classes only. However, more recently, there has been an expansion of such schools, especially preschools and primary schools, and less expensive options have emerged. In fact, labeling a school "bilingual" has become a marketing strategy for highly profitable schools and has been used to define a wide variety of scenarios, ranging from half of the program taught in English to only 4 hours a week of English in the curriculum, which does not truly constitute a bilingual curriculum. Lured by the prospect of their children becoming native-like in English, parents enroll them at the age of 3 or 4, a very young age in such programs.

At the high school level, another recent initiative that has grown exponentially involves the partnership of Texas Tech University and prominent high schools in the country, whereby students complement their Brazilian high school studies with a U.S. curriculum, receiving at the end of 3 years both a Brazilian and a U.S. high school diploma.

Regarding the teaching of English in federal universities, upon realizing that many Science Without Borders candidates were going to Portugal due to their lack of proficiency in English, the federal government in Brazil created a program called English Without Borders, which includes online and face-to-face English classes at universities, free of charge. The program aims to make structural changes in the teaching of English in public and private universities around the country. The online program is available to students in all 2,314 public and private higher education institutions in Brazil, while the face-to-face program is available in 43 federal universities (Ministry of Education, 2013).

Conclusion

Brazil is part of the expanding circle of users of English (Kachru, 1985), and the need for proficient speakers in the academic field and professional market is growing. The government has been unable to provide effective English language instruction in most of the public schools, attended by 83% of the population (Instituto Nacional de Estudos e Pesquisas Educacionais Anísio Teixeira, 2013). Likewise, the vast majority of private schools—attended by the other 17%—are also not capable of teaching EFL effectively due to a number of limitations and their primary focus on university entrance exams that do not require a high level of English proficiency. As a result, ELT has become a very profitable and competitive business in the country, which sometimes compromises the quality of the instruction offered. Binational centers, which used to be the sole providers of EFL classes outside of regular schools, now face fierce competition and have had to adapt their practices to the existing context. Nevertheless, their status as nonprofit institutions is still a competitive advantage and they are also still recognized based on their academic excellence. A major challenge faced by public and private schools, as well as ELT institutes, is the lack of proficient and qualified teachers.

English Language Teaching and Learning at the Local Level in Brazil

According to the Brazilian constitution, the federal government is responsible for organizing and financing the federal educational system and also for establishing curricular parameters for all subjects. Thus, the same laws and policies mentioned in Chapter 2 apply to education in Brasilia.

This chapter starts with a brief history of English language teaching (ELT) in Brasilia, followed by an analysis of the current scenario regarding ELT in public and private schools as well as for adults.

A Growing Demand for English in a Growing City

Brasília was founded in 1960 to become the capital of Brazil. Already present in the 1891 constitution, the plan to build a capital in the central region of the country was made concrete by President Juscelino Kubitschek. The urban planner Lucia Costa and the architect Oscar Niemeyer were hired to design the modern city and its buildings, respectively. The first inhabitants in the city were the public servants transferred from the former capital of Rio de Janeiro, diplomatic missions, and small-scale entrepreneurs willing to take risks and open their businesses in a new city.

Soon after the founding of Brasilia, in 1960 a branch of the Rio de Janeiro Cultura Inglesa was opened. In 1963, Casa Thomas Jefferson was also opened, and for a few years these two traditional institutions remained as the only ELT institutes in the city. In 1973, a third ELT institute called Independent British Institute (Instituto Britânico Independente) opened its doors, founded by former Cultura Inglesa teachers and focusing on British English.

In the late 1960s and early 1970s, with the steady growth of the new capital, branches and franchises of other ELT institutes were established in the city and the market became more diversified. The opening of the country to international markets, promoted by President Kubitschek, contributed to the large growth in the teaching of foreign languages, especially English (Romanelli, 1978). Contrary to Cultura Inglesa, Casa Thomas Jefferson, and Independent British Institute, considered the three traditional ELT institutes in the city, having consistently focused on the development of the four skills, some of these other language programs purported to focus primarily on the development of oral skills.

In 1975, an important step toward the democratization of the teaching of foreign languages in the city was taken with the inauguration of the first Centro Interescolar de Línguas (CIL; Inter-School Language Center). This innovative initiative by the local government aimed to provide public school students with the opportunity to learn foreign languages in an environment similar to that of private language institutes. It is a unique model in the country, since the only state that offers extracurricular foreign language classes, São Paulo, does not offer an infrastructure solely dedicated to the teaching of foreign languages, but rather foreign language classes inside some of its regular schools (Damasco, 2012). This first CIL, named CIL Brasília, was and still is hosted by one of the largest public high schools in the city but has its own dedicated area.

In 1984, a second CIL was opened, this time in Ceilândia, one of the so-called satellite cities of the Federal District. Ten years later, a third CIL in another satellite city was founded, followed by two others in 1995, one in 1996, and two more in 1998. Some of these centers taught English, Spanish, and French from the beginning, while others taught only English or only English and French. Besides offering foreign language instruction to the public school student population, until 2004 the CILs also offered limited spots to the community by way of a highly disputed ballot. However, in 2004 the Secretariat of Education of the Federal District determined that the CILs should offer foreign language instruction only to public school students (Damasco, 2012).

Sant'Anna (2009) conducted a case study to analyze how the second CIL, on the outskirts of the Federal District, was created and shows that its success was due to the personal and individual effort of a group of teachers, not due to a clear and well-established public policy. Without a public model or specific guidelines for public language centers to follow, they adopted the same model as the private ELT institutes, dividing students into levels and adopting international textbooks. Even the funding of the CILs has been unconventional, since improvements in infrastructure and purchase of materials and equipment are funded by money donated to the Parent-Student-Teacher Association. Sant'Anna concludes by stating that the CILs sprang from an informal public policy that emerged from the society itself, not from the local government. He also emphasizes that the CILs provide the low-income population with a unique opportunity to learn foreign languages and improve their professional situation, and thus their social condition.

Another relevant initiative aimed at widening the access to foreign language learning was the creation of the Universidade de Brasília (UnB) Language School, in 2000, with a view to providing foreign language instruction to the university's student population and the community at large for a much lower cost than the tuition in most private ELT institutes. This was possible because of the nature of its extension program, which allows for the recruiting of teachers as service providers, rather than regular employees, exempting the program, part of the university's Extension Program portfolio, from paying the heavy labor taxes levied in Brazil. This program, now called UnB Idiomas (UnB Languages), is provided within the university, is run by the Department of Languages, and serves a population of more than 15,000 students a year, offering over a dozen languages.

Yet a third initiative that is geared toward lower income students and has provided access to English language instruction to students outside Brasilia per se, in the satellite cities, is a cooperative of English teachers called Cooplem (Cooperative of teachers for the teaching of modern languages), founded in 1999. It currently has over 130 teachers, 10 branches, and 9,000 students (see www.cooplemidiomas.com.br).

English Language Teaching in Brasilia Today

The Federal District now has a little over two million inhabitants and more than a hundred ELT institutes, some with multiple branches, offering EFL to different age and proficiency levels, for a variety of prices, and also adopting a variety of methodologies. Seventy-four percent of students at the primary, secondary, and technical education level attend public schools and thus start learning English at school in the sixth grade, with two contact hours a week. Around 30,500 of the public school students in sixth grade or above were learning English in one of the CILs in 2013. A small proportion of public school students are enrolled in private ELT institutes, especially those that cater to the C class mentioned in Chapter 2, an emerging middle class that has been expanding its spending capabilities and gaining access to services and products that were not affordable in the past. The other 26% of students attend private schools, usually initiating English instruction in the first grade, with one 50-minute class a week. From sixth grade on, the contact hours are generally two 50-minute classes a week.

The Federal District is the federal unit that pays the highest salary to teachers in the country, so certified English teachers are attracted by a teaching job in regular schools, not only because of the salary but also because of stability and an attractive retirement plan. An additional attraction is the possibility to teach in a CIL rather than in a regular school. Usually the most qualified and proficient teachers are assigned to the CILs due to the English-only, communicative nature of their classes.

The 26% of students who attend private schools generally begin English language instruction in first grade, though it is only legally mandatory from sixth grade on. Even so, the large groups with mixed abilities and the emphasis on grammar, vocabulary, and reading make it virtually impossible to acquire communicative competence in English only at school, forcing families to also invest in private ELT institutes.

Around the turn of the 21st century, private schools felt the need to improve the quality of their EFL instruction and adopted different strategies. A few opened their own language centers and began offering supplementary classes for an additional fee, according to a private ELT institute model. Others outsourced this service to ELT institutes, either with teachers from these institutes going to their schools to teach the regular English classes or in an afterschool model in which the ELT institutes offer their own courses inside the school and have a small operational infrastructure to support students and teachers.

Casa Thomas Jefferson was a major player in this new model, signing its first contract with a school in 2000 to teach its regular English classes. The advantage for the school was that it would not have to recruit and train English teachers or select appropriate materials, a difficulty most schools have because their principals and executive directors rarely know more than basic-level English themselves and therefore feel incapable of managing the quality of their English curriculum. Thus, outsourcing this service to a reputed ELT institute seemed more advantageous than hiring an English coordinator.

In 2007, Casa Thomas Jefferson partnered with two schools, one of which has three campuses in the city and around 2,000 students, for a much bolder initiative: to teach its own curriculum, with the same class hours, materials, and teachers, in lieu of the traditional English classes. The schools' regular class hours were extended twice a week to accommodate the extra time dedicated to English instruction, and in the last two class periods of the day, all students started having their English classes simultaneously, divided not by their school grade, but according to their proficiency level. This was a turning point for Casa Thomas Jefferson and its teachers because, for the first time, teachers would leave the institution's campuses to go where the students were, and not the other way around. One of these schools has changed hands twice and is now owned by a large conglomerate that also owns two ELT franchises. However, Casa Thomas Jefferson is still in charge of the EFL instruction of all students.

However, not many schools in Brasilia can adopt the model mentioned above because they do not have enough space to simultaneously allocate their students in different classrooms with up to 18 students, since their own classes can have up to 35. Thus, another model that is now very popular was started in 2008, when Casa Thomas Jefferson opened what we call an *outpost*, or a mini-branch, inside two private schools. In this model, Casa Thomas Jefferson (CTJ) is a service provider inside the school and has its own registrar's and coordination office. The families sign a contract directly with CTJ and their children take the same courses taught in the CTJ branches for a monthly tuition around 15% lower than the tuition they would pay in one of the CTJ branches. Casa Thomas Jefferson now has outposts in eight schools, some of which have more than one campus in the city. Other ELT institutes also offer classes inside schools.

This model is very advantageous to parents in a school system that does not operate full time, as they no longer have to pick up their children from school at midday, take them home for lunch, and then drive them or have them take a school bus to an ELT institute. The students can have lunch at school and then engage in their extracurricular activities, the Casa Thomas Jefferson English classes being one of them. Some schools even exempt students learning English at CTJ or any other private ELT institute from attending the regular, mandatory English classes, as long as they present their report cards for the transfer of grades and attendance.

Another segment that has been growing in the city is bilingual or international schools. The most traditional international school in the city is the American School, offering a U.S. curriculum and attended by an international population working at embassies or international agencies, or by Brazilian A and B class students whose parents can afford the very high tuition. Operating in Brasilia since 1980 and with a high tuition, albeit not as high as the American School, is the School of the Nations, a nonprofit bilingual school. More recently, though, other bilingual schools have opened, attracting families who want their children to be native-like English speakers. One of them is the Canadian franchise Maple Bear.

Brasília has a special characteristic, namely, that a great proportion of its working population consists of public servants. There are not major industries or corporations in the city, which makes the corporate contracts for teaching English in-company more directed to the public service and toward general English rather than English for specific purposes. When a government institution such as a ministry or agency needs to hire an ELT institute, it has to initiate a bidding process in which the institution offering the service for the lowest price wins. Hence, there are ELT companies focused primarily on serving the government, hiring teachers on temporary contracts and, thus avoiding the heavy labor taxes that companies with a permanent staff have to pay. A common policy adopted by two large corporations, the Bank of Brazil and Caixa Econômia Federal, is to allow employees to choose where to study English, as long as they provide proof of language acquisition by way of one of the recognized international proficiency tests. Casa Thomas Jefferson has contracts with government offices and agencies due to a law that allows the government to hire nonprofit educational institutions of renowned quality without a bid.

Another important feature of the public service tradition of the capital of Brazil is the constant offering of public service entrance exams for the legislative, judiciary, and executive branches, which attract a large number of applicants because of the high salaries, stability, and advantageous retirement plan. Most of these tests assess knowledge of English by way of reading comprehension, so there is an interest in English classes for the purpose of passing these types of exams, which are also adopted by some departments in the University of Brasilia to assess the English proficiency of graduate program candidates.

Conclusion

Brasilia is the city in Brazil with the highest gross domestic product per capita, and the Federal District ranks as one of the federation units with the highest education standards. The percentage of students attending private schools in Brasilia is higher than the national average. Thus, the city has a promising market for private EFL instruction, attracting numerous franchises offering a variety of models. Proficient and qualified EFL teachers are highly sought after and can choose the type of institution to work for among many options, such as public or private regular schools, more traditional institutions, franchises, cooperatives, university language centers, or even private classes. Some teaching jobs require a national certification, such as jobs in public and private regular schools, while most jobs in private ELT institutes do not require such certification, though it is preferred.

4

Our LTO

Casa Thomas Jefferson, also known as the Casa, is currently the largest binational center in Brazil, with around 17,500 students and 260 teachers. Its mission is to enable the community to communicate effectively in English in a globalized world. In addition to their English programs, binational centers are also expected to engage in educational advising by way of an Education USA office, provide access to published and electronic resources in English by way of a library, and maintain a host of cultural activities for the community free of charge. These activities range from art exhibits, movie showings, and concerts to book launches, debates, and other activities.

Casa Thomas Jefferson serves a large and generally middle-class clientele in a variety of venues: the six Casa Thomas Jefferson campuses, 12 outposts—or mini branches—in regular elementary schools and high schools, corporate situations, courses in government organizations (e.g., Department of Mines and Energy), and even a few private classes. The ages and levels of students range from kids (4–6 years of age) through junior, teens, intermediate, and advanced courses to pre-Michigan and TOEFL testing courses. Adults-only courses cater to the needs and schedules of students over 18 from basic through advanced levels.

The Structure of the Organization

A Board of Directors oversees the nonprofit organization that is Casa Thomas Jefferson. This directing body is composed of professionals from a variety of fields, such as education, law, economics, and business administration. The institution's funding comes primarily from student tuition. Because the institution has close ties with the U.S. Department of State, it receives small and occasional grants from the Department of State or the U.S. Embassy to carry out educational and cultural projects programmed by the Embassy and to improve its infrastructure and technological resources.

The hierarchical structure of the institution consists of an executive director, or CEO, who directly oversees the academic and the administrative and financial superintendents. Under the administrative and financial superintendent are administrative offices such as accounting, human resources, and information technology. Reporting to the academic superintendent are the academic coordinators, who run each of the six branches, and deputy coordinators. Also directly linked to the academic superintendent are the head of the Supervision Department, the head of the Educational Technology and Communication Department, the school psychologist, the Education USA Office, and the Testing Department. The people who occupy the positions reporting to the Academic Department are former teachers who demonstrated leadership skills, as Casa Thomas Jefferson does not hire professionals from outside CTJ for the positions of coordinators or supervisors. These positions are always occupied by teachers who have made their careers within the institution. This is a characteristic that makes CTJ distinct and differentiates it from other ELT institutes.

Each of the six branches of Casa Thomas Jefferson is managed by an academic coordinator, who is responsible for overseeing all the academic work in the branch, providing assistance to teachers, students, and parents. The larger branches have one or two deputy coordinators serving as adjuncts to the academic coordinator. Linked to the various branches are the school outposts, which are mini-branches located within the regular schools where Casa Thomas Jefferson manages its English courses. Each outpost is overseen by an academic assistant or deputy coordinator.

The head of the Supervision and Teacher Selection Department oversees the work of 10 course supervisors. The head of the Educational Technology and Communication Department is responsible for two major tasks: supporting the use of state-of-the-art educational technology in the classroom and online as well as managing the digital communication of the institution. Casa Thomas Jefferson also benefits from the services of a school psychologist and an assistant school psychologist.

The academic superintendent oversees the school libraries, the Educational Advising Office, and the Testing Department, responsible for administering the TOEFL, the Institutional TOEFL, the University of Michigan's Examination of Proficiency in English, and others.

The Courses Offered, the Curriculum, and Course Supervision

The courses offered range from Kids Fun, Kids, and Top Kids, for children ages 4–7; Junior, for ages 8–10; Teens, ages 11–14; and Young Adults/Adults, ages 15 or older, divided into Basic, Intermediate, and Advanced levels. Each of the three latter segments is composed of four sublevels. A student who joins the program at the age of 15 as a true beginner will take 6 years to finish the whole program, with four contact hours a week. Students who start at a young age are placed in the next age segment either when they complete the course (e.g., Junior) or when they reach the maximum age for the course. Typically, a student who starts at Junior 1 will take around 7 years to complete the whole cycle and finish the Advanced course at the C1 level according to the Common European Framework of Reference for Languages (CEFR).

There is also a program exclusively for adults, with three 2-year courses: Thomas Flex, Top Flex, and Thomas Prime. In addition, the course portfolio includes test preparation courses and other types of English for specific purposes (ESP) programs, such as Conversation and Translation Studies.

Online courses comprise general English courses from the Basic to the Intermediate levels and Business English for the Advanced level. These are offered in partnership with two content providers. There are also online ESP courses, such as Practical Writing, Academic Writing, Legal English, Grammar Up, and English for Travel. With the exception of English for Travel, all ESP courses were developed in-house and are delivered via the Moodle learning management system.

In addition, the institution offers university-level Teacher Development courses to in-house teaching staff and those placement-tested applicants wishing to add to their professional credentials and general professional know-how.

CTJ adopts teaching materials that are produced for English language teaching worldwide and that linguistically reflect the use of different varieties of English around the globe, but with a more U.S. than British slant in terms of cultural emphasis, pronunciation, spelling, and so on. However, teachers are encouraged to use supplementary resources and materials, especially authentic ones. When we feel a textbook needs more solid supplementation, we develop handbooks that students purchase together with their textbooks.

Standardization of curriculum and materials is crucial in a large institution like Casa Thomas Jefferson because, unlike intensive English programs or other short-term programs, we are responsible for taking students from the true beginner to the advanced level in an EFL environment, that is, where students are not exposed to English all the time. Students change groups and even branches frequently and expect a continuation of their studies in the group where they initiated their study. This makes it necessary for teachers to use the same core materials at more or less the same pace. That does not mean, though, that they have to follow a prescriptive plan. Within the boundaries of the materials to be used and the schedule to be followed, teachers plan their classes according to their individual style and students' needs, as long as our teaching standards are adhered to.

All courses are supervised by senior teachers with the proven, time-tested qualifications and experience necessary for that task. They direct the adoption of material chosen for the level, create the assessments that—at stipulated times during the semester—measure competency in the level, screen and produce extra exercises and support material for the course, and produce the schedules that determine the timing of each phase of the course until the final exam period. Nevertheless, teacher input in this textbook selection and development of materials is highly valued and encouraged.

Course supervisors also develop all the assessment instruments used for their levels. In the courses for children ages 4–7 (Kids Fun, Kids, and Top Kids), there are no formal assessments. After each teaching period, parents receive a list of learning outcomes worked on and qualitative comments from the teachers.

In the Junior course (8–10 years of age), there are six objectives for each teaching period, comprising 5–6 weeks. Students are assessed according to their accomplishment of each objective. If they do not achieve one of the objectives, they do not have to retake all the assessments, just the one related to the objective not achieved. This allows parents to keep track of their children's progress more closely and allows teachers to reassess students in a more formative manner.

From the Teens course onward, students take a test after each 5- to 6-week period. Our tests are developed by the supervisor because the tests that accompany the textbook series we adopt involve more recognition than production and do not focus on the four skills. Therefore, the tests provided by the publishers are not used. Our in-house tests, on the other hand, necessarily have a listening task, a reading task, language use, and vocabulary. They are also contextualized and balanced regarding selected and constructed-response types of items. These tests are analyzed by teachers in meetings prior to their administration and are administered by all teachers of the level. Thus, teachers do not develop their own tests, but they provide constant feedback to supervisors on the tests developed.

The grading system also considers other aspects, such as class participation and written work. The latter consists of shorter exercises selected by the teachers and completed in class or at home. Class participation is assessed by way of specific rubrics that encompass quantitative and qualitative aspects in students' oral production as well as a few behavioral standards. They are specific to each level and each grading period because they also include the learning outcomes. From the Intermediate level onward, the grade for written work focuses on a piece of writing that is developed throughout the 5- to 6-week period, from planning, to drafting, to revising. Students from the Teens course onward also take an oral test at the end of the semester that covers what was learned during the semester. Specific rubrics also are used to assess students and currently follow a "can-do" format similar to that of the CEFR.

The assessment system in the adult courses (Flex, Top Flex, and Prime) has recently been changed from a summative to a formative one. With a view to shifting the focus from grammar to the assessment of the four skills in a more communicative way, placing greater emphasis on speaking, and in order to lower students' anxiety about final tests, an system was designed whereby students take six short assessments, preferably focused on the four skills with grammar and vocabulary embedded, during the whole module.

Students are assessed by learning outcomes, and these assessments are closely aligned with the learning outcomes proposed and the instructional strategies used to achieve these outcomes. Two of the six assessments are always speaking assessments, with a more informal focus than traditional oral tests. At the end of the module, there is a day when students can retake the assessments whose outcomes they did not achieve or take the ones they missed. This is a way to harmonize the formative assessment system and the need for standardization in such a large institution. This assessment system has been a paradigm shift within the institution and it has been a challenge for some teachers to adapt to it, due to the growing dominance of summative and standardized types of assessments in Brazil.

Educational Technology and School Psychology

In addition to receiving orientation from course supervisors regarding the different levels they teach, CTJ teachers also receive constant training and orientation from our Educational Technology Department and school psychologists.

The Educational Technology Department is responsible for the institution's online and blended courses as well as for implementing state-of-the-art technologies in the classroom and training teachers to use this technology. Each school campus has an ed-tech monitor, a teacher responsible for providing one-on-one assistance to colleagues and conducting training sessions. Regular courses and workshops are conducted to familiarize teachers with new technologies and help them implement these technologies effectively in the classroom. A recent initiative has been implementing the use of iPads in the classroom. The Ed-Tech Department coordinator and her team develop strategies to familiarize teachers with tablets and their educational applications and plan activities that are pedagogically appropriate. They are also on the lookout for new applications for the iPads. The department is responsible for maintaining a wiki called CTJ Connected, where teachers share PowerPoints and videos for different levels. The wiki is also used to showcase news in the Academic Department and calls for meetings and other activities.

Very few ELT institutes have a school psychologist. Since Casa Thomas Jefferson has a large number of school-age students, it also has a proportionate number of students with learning differences, around 5% of the school-aged population. The School Psychology Service, composed of a school psychologist and an assistant school psychologist, is responsible for providing orientation to teachers who have students with learning differences and adapting assessment instruments to meet these students' needs. Common learning differences are attention deficit hyperactivity disorder, dyslexia, Asperger syndrome, and others. The fact that we teach the English curriculum in two regular schools increases the number of students with such difficulties, as some of them would not otherwise be enrolled in an extracurricular English class.

The Teachers

Casa Thomas Jefferson employs almost 250 teachers, including trainee teachers who work with just a few groups of students; "coachee" teachers, who are newly hired teachers undergoing initial diagnostic observations for the purpose of full staff integration, with regular teaching contracts; and teachers with up to 30 years of teaching experience with the Casa (see Table 1).

In general, CTJ teachers have college degrees (or are in the process of degree completion) and internationally recognized certificates of English language proficiency. Many CTJ teachers also have master's degrees in education, English language teaching, linguistics, psychology, or some other field related to language teaching. Most of the teachers have come to the Casa with two or more years of experience in language teaching schools or institutes (teaching private classes is not taken into consideration), and many are well acquainted with the methodological principles based on which CTJ operates.

Of the 246 teachers, only 8 are native speakers of English. It is not easy for the institution to hire native speakers because receiving a work permit in Brazil is a laborious and highly bureaucratic procedure. Moreover, the institution hires teachers with specific TEFL/TESL training and/or teaching experience. Some native speakers who seek jobs with us either do not have any training or experience or, when they do, have difficulty receiving a work permit because they are not married to a Brazilian citizen. When they have a work permit but no experience or training, they are encouraged to join our team of trainees and are hired as regular teachers after 6 months to 1 year if they perform well.

Table 1. Teachers and Their Number of Years at CTJ (July 2014)

No. of years at CTJ	No. of teachers
0–5	152
6–0	24
>10	70
Total	246

Hiring a teacher from abroad for a temporary, 2-year work visa requires obtaining permission from the Ministry of Labor. There is a lot of paperwork involved and CTJ has to justify hiring a foreigner rather than a local teacher. The institution has gone through this process twice, once with a U.S. teacher and once with an Australian teacher. Both were willing to follow the hiring process and wait until it unfolded, which usually takes 6 months to 1 year. The institution is in the process of hiring a company that specializes in recruiting foreign teachers, native or nonnative speakers of English, and taking care of all the paperwork.

To cater responsibly to the needs, desires, and demands of our varied clientele of learners, CTJ's institutional priority is the standardization of linguistic and methodological performance in all classrooms for which CTJ is responsible. Striving for this level of standardization cannot result in perfection, but it does provide a reasonable likelihood of professional synchrony among the staff as a whole and what is close to a guarantee of functional understanding and acceptance of the Casa's general policies and goals. Thus, teacher selection, coaching, and continued professional development are three highly important processes at CTJ.

The Hiring Process

The process of joining the CTJ staff begins with some form of application indicating professional interest and experience, and detailing education and employment background. The application is usually sent electronically to the person in charge of screening teaching candidates. If the information in the application corresponds to basic staff background requirements, the candidate is contacted to arrange a personal interview, during which the information in the application is discussed in more narrative detail and the candidate's oral English proficiency is informally assessed in terms of fluency and accuracy. Questions are also asked of the candidate regarding his or her understanding of professional commitment and institutional engagement.

If the candidate has made a positive impression up to that point, a time is scheduled for him or her to take a more formal, extensive in-house professional proficiency exam. Having achieved a satisfactory test score, the candidate is called to give a sample class, which is a simulation of a real class in which senior teachers play the role of teens or intermediate students using the regular CTJ classroom material. This simulation is one of the most decisive moments in the hiring process. The purpose is to assess the candidate's connection to the students, lesson phase planning and pacing, oral correction strategies, use of the board and other visual devices, and focus on the stipulated learning outcomes. Any teaching candidate who has produced curricular proof of professional preparation and experience in keeping with institutional-level classroom teaching, and who has created a promising impression during the scheduled oral interview, is asked to give this simulation of practical teaching performance. The class is limited to 20 minutes, during which time the applicant demonstrates the academic organization and techniques necessary to introduce or provide practice with material selected from one of the series used in the Casa's regular Junior or Intermediate courses.

The questions following a positive sample class teaching relate to availability: Does the candidate have other employment (with possible conflicting hours)? Is he or she pursuing academic course studies (which could be a similar problem, in terms of availability)? Does he or she face time limitations due to domestic arrangements? The candidate's desirability on one level may be unfortunately offset by influences beyond his or her control, which may make it difficult to match with the Casa's teaching schedule requirements.

Coaching of New Teachers

Once a candidate has received general approval and availability issues have been dealt with, now newly contracted, he or she automatically becomes part of a group of first-timers called *coachees*. Before the semester begins, the coachees receive various levels of orientation by course supervisors and upper level academic administrators; lesson organization, tactics for teaching young children, fundamentals of CTJ methodology, approaches to the teaching of different levels, and so on are offered in preservice sessions. These sessions are intended to situate new teachers with regard to CTJ teaching policies and philosophy, and to help smooth the process of integrating new teachers with the Casa's more senior members.

Among the above-mentioned sessions, attendance at all of which is mandatory, is one with the coaches, a group of pedagogical counselors contracted by the Casa to assist and partner with new teachers in their first weeks of work. These coaches (there are currently four) have been colleagues in various levels of Casa classroom teaching and academic administration for many years. Their focus in their current collaborative position is to first work with the new teachers in the induction process, which usually last 6 weeks. This involves participation in lesson planning, observation of classes on more than one level of instruction (Preteens, Junior, Basic Adult, etc.) and in two or three venues (Casa branches, regular schools, in-company courses, etc.), with a comprehensive analysis of the outcomes of each of the lessons. Once the coachees look and feel secure and effective in a variety of pedagogical situations, they are "green-lighted." This signifies recognition of performance level on par with the institution's regular staff, and it indicates that the coachees are ready for class observation by supervisors, branch coordinators, and other academic administrative personnel.

All incoming teachers should be aware that class observation is, in the first place, a form of support and an incentive in the challenge of adapting to a new environment and to a wide variety of student responses and agendas. Regular summary observation reports, and those following coaching observations, also serve to build up a performance portfolio that is analyzed at the end of every teaching year for the purpose of professional evaluation. This assessment helps class schedule programmers evaluate performance strengths and weaknesses (particularly empathy with small children, tactful motivation of adults who are both busy and anxious, ability or inability to "click" with teens, etc.) in the attempt to situate all staff members, as much as possible, where they can be most effectively and most positively productive.

One of the requirements in the schedules of all new teachers, regardless of their previous experience, is attendance at Friday morning training sessions, another source of support with various academic focuses, which were designed to help ensure new teachers are familiar with both the academic guidelines and institutional procedures in the overall CTJ system.

The period of CV analysis, initial interview, sample class teaching, coaching, and eventual green-lighting is often fraught with unexpected situations, expectations, and occasional frustrations. But it is also infused with and energized by a sense of camaraderie with fellow teaching candidates and coaches. When new teachers have incorporated all the elements described above, when all this information becomes part of their daily routine and their classroom practice, they can finally say they have been fully hired by the Casa.

Continued Professional Development at CTJ

Teacher development is highly valued at Casa Thomas Jefferson, and there are a number of opportunities for teachers to grow professionally within the institution, ranging from short- to long-term initiatives.

The most traditional opportunity for professional development offered by the institution is its Teacher Development course (TDC). It is currently a blended course, with 50% of each semester's curriculum taught online and 50% face-to-face. The course is composed of five semesters, each consisting of 66 hours, focusing on (a) pedagogical grammar; (b) academic writing and phonetics and phonology; (c) second language acquisition, educational psychology, and neuroscience; (d) ELT methodology 1, and (e) ELT methodology 2 and practicum. Student teachers are assessed by way of tests, oral participation, and reflective writings. The reflective writings are compiled in a blog, which constitutes the student's TDC portfolio. Many of the professionals currently working at CTJ took this course and were hired because of their outstanding performance in it.

Another opportunity for professional development is the annual CTJ TEFL Seminar that is open to the teaching community. It is sponsored by the major international publishers established in Brazil and the U.S. Department of State, with many renowned speakers, such as Michael McCarthy, David Nunan, Jeremy Harmer, and Jack Richards, who have presented plenaries and/or workshops. It is a unique opportunity for CTJ teachers to present talks and workshops to their colleagues. Many, in fact, have gone on to become popular ELT presenters internationally, after having started presenting in the CTJ TEFL Seminar. Thus, CTJ teachers do not necessarily have to travel abroad to gain access to the most renowned professionals in the field of ELT and to stay abreast of the latest trends.

Casa Thomas Jefferson also sponsors teachers who present in the national Braz-TESOL conference, held every 2 years, and in the TESOL International Association and IATEFL conferences. In 2014, for example, CTJ sponsored the participation of eleven presenters at the TESOL International Association conference and one at the IATEFL conference. At the most recent Braz-TESOL event, there were eight presentations sponsored by CTJ. Teachers who present at these events are also required to share their experience in these events with their colleagues, either by presenting in the yearly CTJ TEFL Seminar or by writing a post for the CTJ Connected wiki.

The CTJ Connected wiki is yet another opportunity for teachers to share their expertise with their colleagues. It was created in 2009 but was maintained only by the ed-tech monitors. In 2012, it was relaunched with a new identity: to showcase posts from all teachers on a variety of topics of their interest. Since the relaunch, and as of July 2014, there have been over 80 posts by more than 30 teachers on a variety of topics, including classroom management, educational technology, methodology, practical ideas for the classroom, book reviews, and others.

Teacher Observation and Annual Evaluation

Casa Thomas Jefferson has had a systematized teacher supervision and evaluation system since the late 1980s. Every teacher is observed three to four times a year by different supervisors, coordinators, deputy coordinators, and four academic consultants who are also new teachers' coaches. The observation process follows the pre-observation, observation, and post-observation cycle and reflection is a key component. The process results in a filed observation report, in the form of a checklist comprising these standards: planning; instructing; learning; assessing; interpersonal dynamics; language, culture, and digital literacy; attention to rules and procedures; and investment in professional development (in this case, by way of active participation in the pre- and post-observation process). They are the same standards that constitute a document titled *Standards for Casa Thomas Jefferson Teachers,* which enumerates the nine standards set forth by the Casa, with detailed indicators. This document was adapted from the *Standards for EFL/ESL Teachers of Adults* (TESOL International Association, 2008).

Teachers' performances are evaluated yearly, and the eight standards listed above are addressed. A ninth standard not mentioned above is professional attitude and commitment. The evaluation document contains the nine standards and descriptors for each level of performance: exceeds the standard, meets the standard fully, meets the standard most of the time, meets the standard partially,

PERSPECTIVES ON TEACHING ENGLISH IN A BINATIONAL CENTER IN BRAZIL and does not meet the standard. The observation report also contains these categories, with the exception of exceeds the standard.

Information resulting from teacher evaluation is used for decisions regarding academic positions, awarding of bonuses and grants, selecting peer mentors, and other matters. More important, the evaluations are used to inform CTJ about what to address in its continuing professional development programs.

Teacher supervision and evaluation have been the backbone of the Casa's academic excellence. Teachers are encouraged to invest in their professional development and value the opportunities for growth that CTJ provides. The Casa, in turn, is able to keep track of performance and allocate resources to areas that are observed as lacking expected quality.

Casa Thomas Jefferson and Other Binational Centers in Brazil

There are 62 binational centers in Brazil, some smaller, others larger, some for-profit, others nonprofit. CTJ shares many more similarities than differences with the larger binational centers that are also nonprofit. We selected three of these nonprofit institutions, located in different regions of the country but all in large capital cities, to offer some comparative data, as shown in Table 2.

Most binational center students are under 18 years of age, and all the binational centers (BNCs) listed in Table 2 have programs for very young learners, demonstrating that children in Brazil are now beginning their EFL experience younger and younger. Another common trend is to open branches, what we call outposts, in regular schools, adapting to the changing needs of learners.

Yet another aspect common to all these BNCs is the predominance of nonnative speakers of English who are teachers on their staff, due to a number of factors already discussed in this chapter. Nevertheless, all teachers are highly proficient in English, and the lack of a large number of native speakers on our staff does not seem to pose a problem for students.

These BNCs are also similar in their choice of skills-integrated, international textbooks and adoption of a communicative approach to teaching EFL. Investment in teachers' professional development is also a priority among these centers. In fact, the BNCs in Rio, São Paulo, and Salvador began offering a TEFL Seminar long before CTJ did, which inspired us to follow suit.

The BNCs in Rio, Salvador, and São Paulo also offer Portuguese for foreigners, a course that CTJ is planning to introduce in the near future, again inspired by our counterparts. There are some other similarities among the BNCs, especially regarding the types of ESP courses and online or blended programs offered. Even so, the core courses are very similar in their objectives, materials, methodologies, and numbers of contact hours.

Table 2. Comparative Data for Five Binational Centers in Brazil (July 2014)

Institution	No. of teachers	No. of pedagogical staff (course supervisors, branch coordinators, managers, etc.)	No. of native-English-speaking teachers	No. of students	Percentage of students under 18	Lowest age of entry	Outposts in regular schools
Casa Thomas Jefferson, Brasília	246	30*	8	17,400	74%	4	12
Associação Alumni, São Paulo	109**	8	3	5,300	57%	4	7
ACBEU Bahia, Salvador	70	8	5	5,200	70%	4	4
CCBEU, Belém	36	6	2	3,800	68%	2	1
Ibeu Rio	255	25***	8	15,000	70%	3	21

*Not all are full-time.

**100 English teachers and 9 translation teachers.

***One academic supervisor is part-time; branch managers perform a more administrative role.

A Day in the Life of a Teacher in Our LTO

Beginning the Day

Very momentarily, the teacher resists the alarm, which signals the start of another very busy day. On any given day, this person is responsible for at least two teaching levels—perhaps Teens and Intermediate or Juniors and one Adult group—in one or two regular schools and one CTJ branch or campus. One priority is to go over the itinerary of teaching locations and the plans for each class. The Casa's standards with regard to class planning and delivery are both demanding and specific, and the teacher has to be in command of the appropriate strategies for the achievement of every lesson goal and the particularities of each teaching venue. The teacher also has to be sure that tests, compositions, and exercises have been corrected in accordance with supervisory directives (the teacher's eventual performance evaluation takes these things into account), and an administrative checklist includes keeping up to date with the school's secretarial offices regarding grades and the registry of student absences and/or tardiness. It is also important that the requested and/or pre-prepared materials (including PowerPoint, flash drive) be ready and coordinated with the groups for which they were intended—are the right materials and books for that day in the teacher's bag?

In another early-morning bedroom in the Federal District, another teacher could be temporarily putting scholastic planning on hold (having burned quite a bit of midnight oil on it the night before) while making sure the domestic priorities are being observed (like getting children respectably clothed, fed, and reassured of limitless—albeit hurried—affection, and in readiness for the transfer of domestic care to the maid, nanny, or mother-in-law, or perhaps the arrival of the local school bus). During the day, there might be coordinated inclusions of children's (or personal) swimming classes, piano lessons, or art classes, which are strategically aligned with the teacher's own CTJ class schedule. Most teachers live in apartments. These relatively confining circumstances often create a yearning for activity provided by exercise gyms, Pilates programs, walking, and jogging. Central Brasília is fairly flat and well shaded by an impressive number of trees, so it lends itself to the easy enjoyment of people with dogs or friends who are athletically inclined.

Two considerations have a decisive influence on a teacher's preparation for the day. One is attention to CTJ dress code, the set of stipulations which—although not rigid or regimented—govern the appropriateness of classroom clothing on the teacher's part. Clothing cannot be unkempt, distractingly revealing, or pushing the limit of casual, and this includes footwear. Bermuda shorts, miniskirts, strapless tops, and extreme adornments like nose and lip piercings all are outside the parameter of acceptable in the CTJ context. The other consideration, which is not flexible, is punctuality. Classes, meetings, and events all begin on time, and teachers are expected to be present even a few minutes before the stipulated time. This stricture influences what time a teacher has to leave home to allow for a trouble-free trajectory to the workplace, which might be a few blocks or many miles away and present various possible impediments to a timely trip. The timeliness of any trip to work depends on the time of day, the distance from home to one's first destination, and the mode of transportation—determined by choice or necessity. Brasilia's residents are not known for carpooling, so the main arteries of traffic leading in and out of the central city are generally quite congested from 7 to 9 a.m. and 5 to 7 p.m. There are other transportation alternatives, such as buses and the subway, but traveling by these means usually necessitates extra time for walking from the transit stop to the actual destination in a city that is not pedestrian-friendly. Some teachers are still going to college and have classes either in the morning, before their shift at CTJ, or in the evening, after their shift.

Getting Started at Work

Depending on what day of the week it is, both of these teachers have other events in their busy schedules. An early morning class might be followed by a meeting with a supervisor, coach, or coordinator about an upcoming class observation. If it is a Friday, there might well be a meeting scheduled that offers orientation for test correction procedures, ed-tech upgrading, tips for class management with small children, and so on. Given time and any luck with the traffic, there will be a break for a fortifying lunch—with family or on the run—because *everyone* has a class at 2 p.m. Teachers who have children typically go home for lunch and either pick up their kids from school at midday or drop them off at school around 1:30 p.m., as school in Brazil is still only half a day. Many single teachers, on the other hand, have lunch at CTJ. They either bring their own food or purchase lunch from the snack bar. The teachers' lounges in all campuses are large and have kitchens with utensils, a refrigerator, and a microwave oven. Afternoons are usually bound by the rhythm of the entry and exit bells, the congenial breaks for coffee and cookies in the teachers' rooms, the completion of all the plans so thoughtfully made the day before, and the connections made with all those familiar student faces.

Planning for those connections might include scanning the CTJ Connected wiki's electronic collection of downloadable exercises, activities, and strategic teaching presentations that are available use in the classroom. Planning also includes reviewing the steps the lesson will take and how students might react to them, where pitfalls might appear, what aspects of the lesson might be redirected, and so on. How will the teacher set the tone and spark engagement with the subject or structure in focus? What will be the "jump start" for spontaneous inter-action among the learners? In those last moments of class, how will the teacher wrap up a line of action, a small project development, and leave the students remembering the class positively as more indelible than a "normal" class period?

All Casa teachers are encouraged to view lesson plans in much the same way as a pilot sees a flight plan, a necessary guide to the connections in coherent per-formance, with an expected outcome clearly in mind. From their initial integra-tion with the staff and Casa teaching procedures, the teachers are provided with a variety of lesson plan templates and are free to choose the one that represents the greatest degree of convenience and clear direction. The important thing is to have a plan at all times, which serves as a kind of GPS as a class progresses and a handy reference in reviewing what was actually accomplished during the period.

Handling a Varied Schedule

Teachers' schedules range from 20 to 40 hours of teaching per week. Teachers with more than 28 hours a week in the classroom receive two preparation hours, and many of them have two or four stand-by hours. These are times when teachers have to be available for substitutions or other academic activities, such as tutoring students with difficulties or administering a placement test. Because CTJ has classes Monday to Thursday from 7:30 a.m. to 9:30 p.m., including a few groups at lunchtime, teachers' work schedules vary considerably. Some may teach an early adult class, followed by a class in a partner school, take a lunch break, and then return to CTJ in the afternoon to teach from 2 to 6. Others may not teach in the morning and only start at lunchtime or at 2 p.m., working until 8 or 9:30 p.m. There are few classes on Fridays, and they are usually in the afternoon. Saturdays mornings, on the other hand, are very busy on all campuses, so around 70% of CTJ teachers have Saturday morning groups, comprising either young adults and adults or very young learners aged 4 to 6. One of the branches also has adult groups on Saturday afternoon.

Newly hired teachers almost always teach on two or three CTJ campuses or outposts and usually have to drive or take a bus from one location to another on the same day. When this is the case, they receive a transportation allowance. In subsequent semesters, though, academic coordinators make an effort to assign classes to teachers on the same location each day, so when teachers work on different campuses, it is usually on different days of the week (e.g., Mondays and Wednesdays at one campus or outpost and Tuesdays and Thursdays at another).

A distinctive characteristic of CTJ is that most of its teachers teach different age and proficiency levels, rather than teaching only adults or only children, for example. It is not unusual for teachers to have groups of young learners at the beginning level as well as groups of post-advanced adults. Most teachers appreciate this variety and are flexible regarding age and proficiency levels. Nevertheless, there are a few teachers who work only with very young learners or who teach mostly adults.

The possible breaks in teachers' schedules, either because of the need to relocate to another teaching venue or because the schedules of different levels result in a time lapse between them, mean that teachers may have time to correct assignments (using standard rubrics and commonly known linguistic terms), fill out report cards, or work on refining a lesson plan for a class later in the day or the day after.

Keeping in Contact With Students and Parents

Teachers also need to find the time to contact the parents of students whose grades are sliding below the requisite average and/or whose behavior or conduct is indicative of a learning difficulty or an attitudinal problem. The students' scholastic data is provided to parents online, by way of a customized platform, but sometimes there might be the need to call parents. This personal connection with a teacher generates cooperative approaches to difficulties and is more likely to result in constructive solutions. On the other hand, teachers might want to transmit congratulations for a student's exemplary participation. Parents should not necessarily see a call from the school or an entry on the student's online profile as being a warning of impending misfortune. Pleasure and pride should be natural returns on investment of energy, time, and financial resources.

Another kind of contact might be periodically helpful to the adult student: an expressed concern about a potentially jeopardizing number of absences, information about a missed assignment or a pending assessment, comments about interests common to the study group as a whole. Teachers usually make themselves available online to Advanced and Adult students by way of private and institutional email. This is often how homework of all kinds is sent, and returned, in completion of regular classroom assignments. Teachers need to reserve a regular block of time to communicate with learners who are more assiduous with their electronic devices than with pencils and tablets. This attention to learners as individuals in teachers' personal care often contributes substantially to students' motivation and continuation in the course.

Finally, a teacher's evening could contain a class on one of various levels, but it always includes reflection on the occurrences of the day. These are the hours for reestablishment of "home," investment in a new romance, lying back with a soap opera or other television series, or perusing Facebook. But at some point the realities of the next day resurface and the teacher's mind inevitably and obligatorily begins to churn with the demands and projected pleasures of tomorrow.

6

A Day in the Life of a Student in Our LTO

Casa Thomas Jefferson has students of all ages, so in this chapter, we will focus first on our largest group of learners, teenagers, and then provide a glimpse of a day in the life of adult students and young learners as well.

Teenagers

Teenagers may not be remarkably different from each other anywhere in the world. Caught in what might feel like an endless stretch of time between infancy and adulthood, they often juggle a relatively two-dimensional existence between free time and time programmed by a legion of directing adults. They get up at what seems to many of them an unreasonably early hour to get ready for school, have a breakfast that will sustain them until a mid-morning snack, and avail themselves of arranged transportation—by car-driving parents or carpooling neighbors, by hired school van or bus—to get to school. Most of our students go to private schools, and each of these high schools or elementary schools has an identifying characteristic, its reputation for being tough, permissive, liberal, and so on, and each casts an advertised net of attractions to appeal to students, parents, or both in an attempt to increase enrollment. Subjects are, in general, studied to be passed and teachers are basically seen as potential pals on a certain level because they have gone through the same experience.

The system exerts considerable pressure on high school students in particular. They take a variety of subjects, sometimes more than 12, and their extracurricular hours are often taken up with a full schedule of programmed activities connected to sports, music, tutoring, foreign language study, and so on. Success in both required and extracurricular engagements is seen as an essential contribution to the accumulation of academic skills necessary to pass highly competitive university entrance exams. These exams considerably narrow the field of who is going to pursue higher education in tertiary institutions whose credentials will be highly regarded in the eventual launching of a career.

Most teenagers learning English at CTJ go to their regular schools in the morning and take English classes at one of our branches or in their regular schools—one of our outposts—in the afternoon. Some go home for lunch, while others have lunch at their own schools. A small number of these students have English classes at CTJ in the morning and attend their regular schools in the afternoon. There are two schools next door to two of our campuses where the mandatory English classes are taught inside CTJ, using our own curriculum and with the same number of contact hours. In this case, the English classes occur during the same period as the regular classes, either in the morning or in the afternoon, so learners do not have to stay at school for an extended period or go to one of CTJ's campuses for their English classes.

What does the average student look for in an English class, whether it is part of a regular school schedule or taken in a separate language school? Teachers know that students hope their English classes will be a different experience in some way, that it won't always seem like a "class." Teachers strive to create the means for linguistic absorption that will stimulate, involve, and be indelible in the long run. Teachers' resources are becoming more sophisticated by the hour, but their efficacy as tools will be proven by students who are actually surprised that the class has already ended, or they will be condemned by youngsters who are following the second hand of the clock on the wall.

In any case, on a daily basis, homework is to be postponed as long as possible and tests are to be crammed for the night before. The challenge is to create a balance between scholastic demands, domestic involvements, urgent electronic communication, and life-saving sleep. All of these dimensions are best confronted in groups and fueled by an extensive provision of snack foods and soft drinks.

Teenagers focus their energy on getting to classes on time, keeping up with assignments, trying not to do things that are "dumb," preventing—as much as possible—parental harassment over issues like cleaning their room. They pay attention to short-term goals, like getting through the week, without losing sight of long-term objectives, like getting through the year. They stay in touch with the central figures in their protective circle, like parents and other relatives, and assiduously revive connections with friends by every electronic means possible during all waking, otherwise unoccupied, moments of the day (which might even involve surreptitious engagement during supposedly occupied moments, such as during an English class).

Every day is experienced on the basis of a virtually protected "independence," with the parameters of their actions determined by family policy and the length of the tether which is the cell phone and its apps. What are you doing, where are you doing it, who are you doing it with? The need to know prevails as much as the need to do, and operational imperatives regulate the force of these two fields at any given time. The daily life of a teenager here is busy, perhaps impacted by conflicting stimulations, and perilously full of the expectations of others with regard to what you should be, and be doing.

Adults

Adult students here sees English study from a different perspective. Whereas teenagers see English as one more subject in a roster of obligatory academic focuses, adults choose English study as instrumentally necessary for employment procurement or retention, career advancement, or personal fulfillment on a variety of levels. Adult learners at CTJ incorporate English classes into an already busy life, fitting them into an early morning schedule before work, taking time for them during lunch hours, or adding them after the regular day's activities in the early or late evening. Adults need to see English as comfortable, fun, and functional. They need to see knowledge of this language as contributing to who they are as people in general, who they are still becoming as local and global citizens. Adult learners have relatively well-defined ambitions, but also very sensitive ego issues, including a fear of sounding infantile, having insecure memory, needing encouragement and praise. Our adult learners need reassurance on a daily basis that the investment they are making will have compensatory returns. The inclusion of English in a day's agenda is a conscious choice, and there are numerous attractions competing for the space occupied by that engagement. A wedding anniversary, a feverish child, an office party, a tension headache. These are elements that are balanced against whether to face the traffic and go to class. Every time adults take that decisive step to enter the classroom, they reaffirm a commitment to themselves, and the decision must continue to seem worthwhile.

Our adult students typically fall on either end of a continuum of interest and effort: the ones who perform only the minimal activities required to pass from one level to the other and the ones who dedicate a great amount of their time to engaging in extracurricular tasks to develop their English proficiency further. The difference is perceived as the years go by and the proficiency gap between the former and the latter becomes more evident. The former typically attend only the number of classes required to pass, rarely do their homework, and often postpone taking tests in order to have more time to study what should have been studied before. The latter group of adults have very high expectations regarding their teachers' knowledge and expertise and will complain to the academic coordinator whenever they feel their expectations are not met.

Many adult students see their English classroom as an opportunity for both learning and socializing. It is not uncommon for groups of adults to become close friends and meet after class or on weekends for leisure or to study for an upcoming test. They many times create What's App or Facebook groups to keep in touch and usually invite the teachers to join in.

Young Children

And last but not least are the kids, from 4-year-olds holding their parent's hand all the way to the classroom door to children of 8 or 9 for whom a great many things constitute either a joy or an emergency and who view themselves as preteens, minutes away from enjoying a long roster of rights and privileges. Depending on their agenda in their schools, they begin their day with an English class twice a week, which takes place mid-morning before lunch or during the afternoon schedule, or they end the day's activities with an English class that has to effectively compete with a forceful desire to congregate with friends or head home to family. In either case, at home they shuck off backpacks in a blessed period of relief . . . before it is time to be reminded that homework should precede the lure of tech communication or TV.

Children nowadays learn English by way of the labels on their clothing, the music on their iPod or cell phone, and the changing names of newer model cars. They learn English by way of very consciously designed materials, those produced by big-name publishers for youngsters around the world and used by teachers in tune with the techniques that will hold the attention of people accustomed to a constant kaleidoscope of stimulation. These kids need to be simultaneously guided and cajoled, given parameters and praised, routed through every day with little left to chance. Most parents consider leaving kids "on the loose" to be potentially dangerous, given the various forms of temptation and predatory influences that can lure children from their programmed path. So, like their other obligations, English classes are held in a situation that is interactive and engaging but also guarded by vigilant monitors and uniformed caretakers of rules and regulations. Since kids naturally react more positively to what they like, the family, society, and schools here go to considerable trouble to provide experiences that are enjoyable, from soft bath towels to warm meals to functional comfort in school furniture to technological facilities of all sorts. Comfort and novelty, balanced with reassuring familiarity, are assessed consistently from morning until night and are judged with a relatively merciless lack of latitude. In Brazil today, children have high expectations, and the investors in their education attempt to meet and satisfy them all.

Parents here have very high expectations for their children, whether young kids or teens, and hope they will develop near-native fluency in English. They expect the language program to engage their children in stimulating activities both in class and at home, and also expect the teachers and academic coordinators to maintain close contact with them regarding their children's activities in class. CTJ has recently invested in a parent-teacher communication platform where teachers have the weekly task of entering information about students' attendance, behavior, and performance in class. This has become one more addition to the teachers' already very busy day, as the previous chapter showed.

7 The Big Picture

When we go to TESOL conferences or other academic events abroad, it is usually difficult to explain to other teachers and academics what Casa Thomas Jefferson is. In countries where the English language teaching (ELT) industry is not as competitive as in Brazil, and where children learn English effectively or relatively effectively at school, an institution dedicated solely to the teaching of English with over 17,500 students is unimaginable. Here are some questions we often hear:

> But what time do your school-age students go to class in your institution? Don't they spend all day at school already?

> But you also teach other subject areas, right? How can such a large school have so many students and teach only English?

Indeed, institutions like Casa Thomas Jefferson, with a very large number of students of all ages learning EFL for a long period of time, are common only in developing countries like Brazil. In many more developed countries, private ELT institutes usually cater to a smaller young adult and adult audience. In those countries, the type of student that attends our institution would probably be enrolled in a bilingual school. In fact, this is already a trend among children from more affluent families in Brazil and will probably extend to the middle class/ C Class in the future.

Thus, in addition to our size and infrastructure, there are many other factors that distinguish our context from other contexts where English is taught around the world. In fact, when attending conferences abroad, it is sometimes difficult for us to find sessions directly related to our specific context. We always benefit from what we see and hear, but we often have to adapt presentation content to our particular situations.

Though we teach the four skills and the subskills of grammar and vocabulary, we are not like an intensive English program that students attend for a short time—months or a year at the most—and from which they go back to their home countries or are mainstreamed in the host country. Despite teaching children as young as 4, we are not a regular school where English and content are taught and children stay for a whole period every day. Especially from the intermediate level onward, we have an ongoing writing program with a process writing approach, but we are not a college or university teaching Writing 101 or Freshman Composition. In fact, we teach writing integrated with other skills. We have a solid teacher education and continued professional development program, though we are not a school of education. Therefore, everything we attend and read about intensive English programs, ESL in K–12, second language writing, and teacher development, to name a few topics, can be only indirectly or partially applied to CTJ.

How We Are Different From Other Organizations

In what ways are we different from other contexts around the world, then? In order to answer this question, we sought help from two U.S. English language fellows who worked at the Casa for 6 months to a year and an Australian teacher who spent 2 years at the institution. We felt that we needed to see CTJ from the standpoint of educators who had been and are now again in a different context. These three professionals agreed to provide their input for this chapter and answered a questionnaire by e-mail.

The difference that stands out the most is the size of the Casa compared with most institutions, as pointed out by Courtney Pahl, of Oregon State University:

> Casa is a much larger school/program than most other ESL/EFL contexts. In the United States, I recently worked for Oregon State University, which has one of the largest ESL programs in the United States (if not the largest) and we have approximately 1,600 students and about 100 full-time instructors.

Another major difference is that our teachers work with many different ages and proficiency levels. They do not teach only children, only adults, or only advanced learners. In fact, it is not uncommon for a teacher to have on the same day a group of small children, followed by a group of intermediate-level teens, and finally a third group of advanced adults. As Sophie O'Keefe, an Australian who used to work at CTJ and who is now working at a college in Sydney called Navitas English, says,

> [One] way in which the Casa is different from my teaching context is the variety of classes, levels, age-groups, etc. which educators teach in any one day. In my context, I teach the same group of students every day for the length of their courses. However, at the Casa, something that I found really interesting was teaching such a mix of classes on a daily basis. I remember feeling like I wore many different hats during my days there.

In addition, if they choose to, teachers at CTJ can be involved in a series of extracurricular projects that can broaden their horizons academically and professionally. For example, they can engage in one of the many projects the institution carries out in partnership with the U.S. Embassy, such as the Public Teacher Development Program or the English Access Microscholarship Program. The former is a 1-year, 120-hour program developed locally that is supported by the U.S. Embassy in Brasília and aims to strengthen the teaching of English in public schools by improving teachers' English and methodological skills. The latter is a worldwide program sponsored by the U.S. Department of State, with a view to offering access to high-quality ELT to disadvantaged teens between the ages of 14 and 18, focusing on U.S. cultures, personal and career development, and service learning.

CTJ teachers can also be involved in the administration of proficiency tests such as those provided by the University of Michigan. Senior teachers at CTJ can also be teacher developers and mentor novice teachers, and they can participate in study-abroad fairs and collaborate with our Education USA office by giving workshops on how to write college application essays, for instance. In sum, an institution with so many activities and dimensions can enrich a teacher's experience in a way that smaller and more specialized ones cannot.

Another distinctive aspect is that we are a very large institution, but we are not part of a franchise network or a network of schools. We are a local institution with the independence to change our curriculum and materials as we see fit. We are also an institution where the key people in leadership positions have been working at CTJ for 30 years (or more) and who started here as teachers.

However, as a large organization that needs standardization, CTJ "controls" teachers in a more systematic manner than in other contexts Courtney Pahl has taught in. She points out that while teachers at CTJ need to submit the extra materials they develop for academic coordinators' or supervisors' approval, teachers in her current U.S. context are much more independent, so they can develop and use their own materials without necessarily having to obtain permission or submit them for third-party revision. She attributes this difference to the fact that CTJ hires less experienced and qualified teachers and trains them on the job, whereas Oregon State, for example, hires only teachers with master's degrees.

Regarding the students, Sophie points out some of the differences between intensive and non-intensive English settings:

I think the main difference is that students at Navitas are all full-time students who are living abroad. This means that the courses are more intensive than those at the Casa, which students usually attend only twice a week for a couple of hours. Both types of courses have their pros and cons, but I sometimes feel that intensive courses do not give lower [level] students enough time to process new information. However, the intensive courses do have the benefit of forcing students to live and breathe English for at least 4 hours a day, which assists their speed of language acquisition.

How We Are Similar to Other Organizations

However, there are many similarities between the Casa and other language teaching organizations around the world. Some aspects that stand out the most are our methodology and the types of materials used.

> As at the Casa, our classes are also conducted using a communicative method of teaching English, and we use international textbooks as the basis of our curricula. In this respect, I think that especially the Thomas Flex lessons at the Casa have a very similar feel to the lessons here. (Sophie)

Courtney also mentioned the use of textbooks as a similarity between CTJ and the two other contexts she has taught in: Oregon State University and a private ELT institute in Chile.

We also identify ourselves readily with other institutions that strive to maintain a leading advantage in the use of cutting-edge educational technologies as well as others that encourage their teachers to stay abreast of current developments in the field by engaging in continued professional development. Both Sophie and Courtney related the workshops and seminars held in their institutions to the ones they experienced at the Casa. Courtney also mentioned that the teacher seminars at Oregon State University are more low-key, as they do not typically recruit internationally renowned figures to present, like we do at CTJ.

As in many EFL contexts worldwide, finding qualified teachers and maintaining them at the institution is a major challenge. Our teaching candidates may have the expected level of English proficiency but not the methodological skills necessary to work in our organization, or vice versa. They are also easily attracted to other job opportunities that may arise, especially in Brasília, where the public service offers high-paying jobs with attractive benefits. For example, an employee with only a high school degree working at the Brazilian Senate, one of the highest-paying jobs in the public service, earns around $5,000 a month, while a novice teacher with a college degree and 30 hours a week in the classroom will be paid around one-third of that at CTJ or even less in smaller language schools. Other government jobs that attract bright young professionals are at the judiciary or the ministries. Besides the attractive salaries, these government positions offer stability and a health and retirement plan.

What Other Organizations Can Learn From Us

Mentoring and continued professional development are two aspects highlighted by our previous teachers as features that could inspire other organizations.

> Finally, I think that the mentoring program for new teachers at the Casa is wonderfully unique and it was something that was an incredibly useful professional development opportunity for me. The idea of having ongoing observations and mentoring by the same person for your first 3 months at

the school to ensure organizational fit is excellent, and I felt that it was a really necessary time for me, especially for learning about teaching younger students. (Sophie)

Amanda Bradford, who used to work at CTJ and now works at Zayed University, in the United Arab Emirates, explained:

What stood out to me (and still does) as the real key to the organization's success is the high caliber of teachers that the organization retains. There were no "duds" in the bunch and paying attention to their model, one can see that this is no accident. The Casa maintains a deep commitment to the quality of their educators in their unique model of building a highly personalized teacher training component into their teacher evaluation process, which I have not seen elsewhere. As several teaching colleagues remarked to me when I worked there, working at the Casa is like having amazing on-the-job training and education for free. They were amazed at the professional growth they had experienced while working there. I saw exactly what they were talking about too, as I have never seen a group of administrators take such a thoughtful, careful, and focused approach toward teacher professional growth and development in the way that CTJ does, all while providing the emotional support that any successful teacher needs to do the challenging job of educating language learners effectively. This incredibly supportive professional atmosphere translates into an almost-catching collegiality among teachers that makes CTJ an environment where teachers want to be and teachers want to stay. And happy, supported, educated teachers, of course, result in happy, supported, educated learners.

Moreover, Casa Thomas Jefferson is recognized for the efficiency with which it is managed. We asked our former teachers what they thought other language teaching organizations could learn from CTJ. Both Courtney and Amanda mentioned management.

As a language teaching professional who has taught in a variety of educational contexts both in the United States and abroad, CTJ stands out to me in several ways and I believe the organization has much to offer as a model for other language teaching organizations in Brazil and around the world. Having taught briefly at the Casa in 2009 as an English language fellow with the U.S. State Department, what I immediately noticed was the level of professionalism that exists in every corner of the organization. The institution appears to run like a well-oiled machine, with every last aspect of the educational experience being carefully attended to—from the physical classroom environment, to the up-to-date language teaching pedagogy, to the incorporation of educational technology, to the streamlined administrative procedures that operate like a highly successful private business in the United States. All of it was impressive. Adopting this level of efficiency and attention-to-detail would surely benefit any [language teaching and learning organization] worldwide, whatever the context. (Amanda)

CTJ could also help other organizations learn about managing a large program, as most programs around the world are not the size of CTJ, so all administrative procedures related to running very large programs would be useful for other larger programs. (Courtney)

Another aspect mentioned by Courtney that puts CTJ at the forefront is its use of educational technology:

CTJ has mastered (in my opinion) the Tech Department! At INTO OSU [Oregon State University], we had a technology advisor and an iPad cart, but we really don't utilize either resource effectively. The tech advisor ends up setting up individual appointments with the less than tech-savvy teachers to help them set up their CMS [content management system] for the term (huge waste of time and expertise). CTJ has found a great system for providing interesting trainings as well as troubleshooting for instructors.

Looking at the Big Picture

"Big" on a national level is an accurate reference to Brazil's territorial dimensions and its relationship to other Latin American countries. That adjective certainly relates closely to Brazil's connection to and involvement with countries around the world; politically, economically, sociologically, and technologically, Brazil exerts considerable influence on the international scene. There are still huge gaps between the destitute segments of Brazil's population and the very well-to-do, and there are too many families eking out their subsistence off parched earth and wizened shrubs, while at the opposite end of the spectrum some families enjoy a very high standard of living, with access to high-quality private education and health care services. In any case, as regards the expansive, and expanding, relationship of English to the country in general, a variety of aspects connect Brazilians on many socioeconomic levels to the language on a daily basis. The main ones are Brazil's commercial interests (especially those related to import/ export), technological prowess in many fields, affinity with various aspects of English-speaking cultures (especially U.S. culture, by way of music, movies, and other media), and constant comparison of lifestyles and values systems. English is part of students' daily lives, and it is generally accepted that English will in some way affect the direction or the context of their future.

Considering all that has been mentioned above, "big" in Brazil also refers to the number of students who accept English as a given in their scholastic schedule and to the number of venues where English study is carried out, including a large number of private schools and a growing number of franchise or chain-based courses. "Big" is the language learning community in Brazil in general and the widespread variety of courses, resources, and materials expanding each year to meet the desires and needs of this agglomeration of learners who include English in their lives by choice and necessity.

In most large urban centers, "big" is also the binational center, Cultura Inglesa, or other institutes with a consistently good reputation that provide the broadest scope of learning opportunities or the most consistent proof of learning achievement over an appreciable span of time. In Brasilia, for example, there are numerous English language courses in operation. Among them, CTJ serves around 17,000 students in on-campus courses, regular school English course inclusions, in-company corporate situations, online or hybrid courses, and other formats. The school itself is big in its scope and the complexities of its organization and management. Catering to small children all the way through to the last stages of adult learning, being able to provide various forms of in-class or distance learning experiences, offering library services, study-abroad counseling, psychological assistance, and a regular calendar of extracurricular events and cultural programs requires truly coordinated synchrony.

In any case, the present is a rapidly evolving condition, and the big picture of schools or institutes like CTJ may predictably become smaller, or more mosaic-like in their proliferation. Public and private schools, as well as colleges and universities, are advancing in their ELT services and methodology, so at some point in the future, school-aged students will not need to attend a private ELT institute anymore. Thus, the nature and even the size of some schools might have to change, organically adapting to the parameters that are unavoidable in urban reconfiguration and the realigning of learning rhythms and language learning goals among students of all ages and at all levels.

How big is this picture for the English language teacher? The teacher preparing for and entering the EFL field today can be either challenged by a daunting variety of learning levels and teaching modes to deal with on a daily basis or comforted by being able to find a niche, or a performance area in which talents and inclinations can find a productive outlet and reciprocal rewards. Some decades ago, a teaching career involved an investment that was accompanied by a vision of longevity in the pursuit of professional development. For some, this may still be so, but the revolving doors in the teaching industry provide for engaging dynamically in more short-range, rather than long-range, efforts in any given teaching situation. The future may contain a vision of the teaching activity but not necessarily a commitment to a particular organization or institute. Thus "big" can involve broad professional commitment—with teaching being the foundation of one's professional life support system—or a partial contribution to a context that embraces other priorities and ambitions. Whatever a teacher's personal choices entail, the teaching of English in a country like Brazil can only be seen as expanding in scope as it accompanies the development of the country overall.

Reflections

We began this book with a historical account of how access to learning English in Brazil has gone from a luxury available to only a few to a necessity, a service more democratically and diversely available to a larger portion of the population by way of an ever-expanding market. We also demonstrated how the English language teaching (ELT) spectrum in Brazil has become more diversified and how the Brazilian government has invested in programs to strengthen the learning of English, especially at the college level. We realize that there is still much that could be improved, in terms of public policies toward ELT, as shown in the statistics on the small number of Brazilians who actually speak English at an intermediate level. We cannot deny, though, that great strides have already been made.

We went on to examine the evolution of binational centers in Brazil and other English language teaching venues here, and their response to developing commercial and political connections, which increasingly gave rise to an evident need for communicative capabilities in English. This aspect showed us clearly how the exigencies of circumstances require a proactive attitude that prompts a dynamic willingness to adopt and implement shifting methodological concepts, new techniques and materials, and an interest in participating in a more global view of the experience of others. This dimension brings into focus how the awareness of others—through conferences, symposiums, colloquia, and other forums—causes examination of one's own institutional policies and academic procedures.

We then provided a detailed analysis of what Casa Thomas Jefferson is, its history, the courses it offers, how it is organized administratively and academically, how it compares to other ELT institutes in Brasília and in Brazil, and how it differs from other ELT programs around the world. With around 17,000 students, CTJ is neither a school, in the sense that it does not teach another subject besides English, nor a higher education institution. It does not have an owner, but it is not a nongovernmental organization that is supported primarily by grants and donations. It is supported by students' tuition. It is a private, nonprofit institution, but it has to be profitable so it can be sustainable.

We presented a detailed description of our teachers' profiles, putting readers in the shoes of CTJ teachers by visualizing what their day is like. We familiarized readers with CTJ students' profiles and how the teaching is influenced by our specific cultural characteristics, such as how English lessons are seen by children, teenagers, and adults. Our reflections on how students live, what pressures they experience, what ambitions their elders (in the case of teens and younger children) have for them, and that they correspondingly have for themselves, certainly contribute to how language learning can be shaped more usefully and more attractively, to be incorporated comfortably and interestingly into their lives. We hope we have been successful in providing sufficient and realistic information to teachers or prospective teachers who would like to come to Brazil and teach English at a binational center. To be honest, it is not the best-paying job in the world, but it certainly offers the opportunity to gain experience in teaching English to students at a variety of ages and proficiency levels. It is also a good job for those who wish to develop professionally, as CTJ and other binational centers in Brazil provide a wide range of continuing professional development opportunities.

We then discussed how binational centers in general, and Casa Thomas Jefferson in particular—once virtually the sole providers of reputable EFL instruction in their communities—have had to adapt to the changing needs of the country and its population, and the fierce competition from other private ELT institutes and services, such as online courses offered from any place in the world. To this end, we have had to expand our portfolio of courses, establish new partnerships, and invest in professional development and innovation to maintain our leading edge.

When we look back at all the changes that have taken place at CTJ in these past 50 years or so, we are surprised by all that has been accomplished. We were so busy getting our jobs done all this time that we had taken this ongoing expansion for granted. Writing this book has raised our awareness of how different CTJ has become from the school both of us arrived at for the first time in the 1970s, one of us as a teacher and the other as a student. Casa Thomas Jefferson has grown from what could be compared to a small family business to a thriving, professionally managed enterprise. Paradoxically, it has not lost its feeling of "home" to those of us who have been part of the institution's history for so long.

Why is that? What is the secret behind what we consider a successful institution that has managed to balance tradition and innovation? We do not hesitate to say it is the people. Teachers who were once novices at CTJ have become the pillars that still uphold the Casa on a firm foundation. Many creative, relatively like-minded students were somehow attracted by the same flame—even though some of them experimented with international relations, law, journalism, and engineering along the way—and came together as a group of even more like-minded teachers who embraced the theories and techniques that had nourished their own studies. In time, some of these professionals became supervisors, branch coordinators, or other singular positions that would have a determining influence on the profile of CTJ. We believe, from having witnessed this development, that a sturdy academic and business foundation can be formed with elements united from the bottom up and consistently cultivating each other's strengths. With balanced administrative direction and a responsible administrative network serving the public, a positive corresponding response from that public is likely to be seen.

Nevertheless, writing this book has also led us to reflect on the challenges ahead. Large ELT franchises have been expanding by acquiring smaller private language schools. International ELT publishing companies are now opening their own language institutes or acquiring existing ones. Private schools have been expanding students' contact hours with English, and some have adopted a bilingual curriculum. Dozens of start-ups providing online ELT services in a wide variety of formats have arisen. In sum, our space as we know it has been shrinking.

These new challenges can be seen as threats or they can be seen as opportunities. We prefer to focus on the latter. When we developed our vision—to enable the community to communicate effectively in English in a globalized world—we made the conscious choice to keep it broad, something that could help us redefine and reimagine what we do, according to our shifting reality. We have had to reimagine and reinvent ourselves in many ways over the years, acquiring the expertise to work with teens, and then young learners, and then very young learners. We embraced e-learning long before any other binational center in Brazil did, and we have been innovative in this aspect ever since. Thus, we feel CTJ will have the strength and expertise to face the challenges enumerated here and turn threats into opportunities.

There is no infallible recipe for stability, but a business or school that enjoys a reputation of long-standing reliability is more likely to have the flexibility to meet challenges, evolve with the trends of the times, and change its face even while maintaining a familiar profile. All work completed in the writing of this book has fostered learning reflection along with memory regarding the nature of English language teaching and how it is construed and constructed by learners, educators, and administrators.

References

Almeida Filho, J. C. P. (2003). Ontem e hoje no ensino de línguas do Brasil [Yesterday and today in language teaching in Brazil]. In C. M. T. Stevens & M. J. Cunha (Eds.), *Caminhos e colheita: Ensino e pesquisa na* área de *Inglês no Brasil* (pp. 19–34). Brasilia, Brazil: Editora UnB.

Azaredo, M. (2014, February 25). Nível de Inglês no Brasil é baixo e país fica em 38 em ranking [English level in Brazil is low and the country is 38th in rank]. *Estadão*. Retrieved from http://www.estadao.com.br

Cox, M. I. P., & Assis-Peterson, A. A. (2008). O drama do ensino de Inglês na escola pública brasileira [The drama of teaching English in Brazilian public schools]. In A. A. Assis-Peterson (Ed.), *Línguas estrangeiras: Para além do método* (pp. 19–54). São Carlos, Brazil: Pedro & João Editores.

Damasco, D. G. (2012). Uma poposta de periodização do ensino de línguas estrangeiras no Distrito Federal: 1959–2012 [A suggested timeline for the teaching of foreign languages in Distrito Federal: 1959–2012]. *Revista HELB, 6*(6). Retrieved from http://www.helb.org.br

de Jesus, F. J. (2013, September 13). Franquias de escolas de idiomas vão faturar R$ 120 bi em 2013 [Language school franchises will earn R$ 120 billion in 2013]. *Edição do Brasil*. Retrieved from http://www.jornaledicaodobrasil.com.br

EF Education First. (n.d.). *EF EPI: EF English proficiency index*. Retrieved from http://www.ef.com/epi

Ferreira, L. M. C. B., & Rosa, M. A. S. (2008). A origem do Inglês instrumental [The origin of instrumental English]. *Revista HELB, 2*(2). Retrieved from http://www.helb.org.br

Instituto Nacional de Estudos e Pesquisas Educacionais Anísio Teixeira. (2013). *Censo da educação básica: 2012* [Census of basic education: 2012]. Brasília, Brazil: Author.

Leffa, V. J. (1999). O ensino de línguas estrangeiras no contexto nacional [The teaching of foreign languages in the national context]. *Contexturas—APLIESP, São Paulo, 4*, 13–24.

Kachru, B. B. (1985). Standards, codification and sociolinguistic realism: The English language in the outer circle. In R. Quirk & H. Widdowson (Eds.), *English in the world: Teaching and learning the language and literatures* (pp. 11–30). Cambridge, England: Cambridge University Press.

Machado, R., Campos, T. R., & Saunders, M. (2007). História do ensino de línguas no Brasil: Avanços e retrocessos [History of language teaching in Brazil: Progress and setbacks]. *Revista HELB 1*(1). Retrieved from http://www.helb.org.br

Ministry of Education. (1998). *Parâmetros curriculares nacionais: Terceiro e quarto ciclos do Ensino Fundamental: Língua estrangeira* [National curriculum guidelines: Third and fourth cycles of elementary school: Foreign language]. Brasília, Brazil: Author.

Ministry of Education. (2013). *Inglês sem fronteiras* [English without borders]. Retrieved from http://isf.mec.gov.br

Moreira, D. (2010, December 12). 17 franquias de cursos de idiomas [17 franchise language courses]. *Exame.com*. Retrieved from http://exame.abril.com.br/pme/noticias/franquias-de-ensino-de-idioma

Nogueira, M. C. B. (2007). *Ouvindo a voz do (pré) adolescente brasileiro da geração digital sobre o livro didático de inglês desenvolvido no Brasil* [Listening to the Brazilian teenager from the digital generation about the English course books written in Brazil] (Unpublished master's dissertation). Pontifícia Universidade Católica, Rio de Janeiro, Brazil.

Nogueira, M. O. (2010). Os centros binacionais Brasil-Estados Unidos: A sua importância na história do ensino de línguas no Brasil [The binational centers Brazil-United States: Their importance in the history of language teaching in Brazil]. *Revista HELB, 4*(4). Retrieved from http://www.helb.org.br

Paiva, V. L. M. O. (2003). A LDB e a legislação vigente sobre o ensino e a formação de professor de língua inglesa [The LDB and the current legislation on education and English language teacher education]. In C. M. T. Stevens & M. J. Cunha (Eds.), *Caminhos e colheitas: Ensino e pesquisa na área de Inglês no Brasil* (pp. 53–84). Brasília, Brazil: Editora UnB.

Rapoza, K. (2012, April 5). Countries with the best business English. *Forbes*. Retrieved from http://www.forbes.com

Rathbone, J. P. (2014, April 15). Fragile middle: Latin American aspirations risk being frustrated. *Financial Times*. Retrieved from http://www.ft.com

Romanelli, O. d. (1978). *História da educação no Brasil (1930/1973)* [History of education in Brazil (1930/1973)]. Petrópolis, Brazil: Ed.Vozes.

Sant'Anna, J. d. (2010). O cisne e o patinho: Esperança e retrocesso na história de um centro público de línguas [The swan and the duckling: Hope and setbacks in the history of a public language center]. *Revista HELB, 4*(4). Retrieved from http://www.helb.org.br

Santos, E. S. (2011). O ensino da língua Inglesa no Brasil [The teaching of English in Brazil]. *BABEL: Revista Eletrônica de Línguas e Literaturas Estrangeiras, 01*. Retrieved from http://www.babel.uneb.br

TESOL International Association. (2008). *Standards for EFL/ESL teachers of adults.* Alexandria, VA: Author.